PENSIONS AND
INDUSTRIAL RELATIONS

*A Practical Guide for All Involved
in Pensions*

Other Titles of Interest

PENSIONS AND INDUSTRIAL RELATIONS

A Practical Guide for All Involved in Pensions

by

HARRY LUCAS, FCIS, FPMI

Pensions Adviser to the General and Municipal Workers Union

PERGAMON PRESS

Oxford · New York · Toronto · Sydney · Paris · Frankfurt

U.K.	Pergamon Press Ltd., Headington Hill Hall, Oxford OX3 0BW, England
U.S.A.	Pergamon Press Inc., Maxwell House, Fairview Park, Elmsford, New York 10523, U.S.A.
CANADA	Pergamon of Canada Ltd., 75 The East Mall, Toronto, Ontario, Canada
AUSTRALIA	Pergamon Press (Aust.) Pty. Ltd., 19a Boundary Street, Rushcutters Bay, N.S.W. 2011, Australia
FRANCE	Pergamon Press SARL, 24 rue des Ecoles, 75240 Paris, Cedex 05, France
WEST GERMANY	Pergamon Press GmbH, 6242 Kronberg/Taunus, Pferdstrasse 1, West Germany

First edition 1977

British Library Cataloguing in Publication Data

Lucas, Harry
Pensions and industrial relations.
1. Pensions – Great Britain
I. Title
331.2'52'0941   HD7106.G8   77–30221
ISBN 0–08–021947–0 (Hardcover)
ISBN 0–08–021946– (Flexicover)

*Typeset by Cotswold Typesetting Ltd., Cheltenham
Printed in Great Britain by William Clowes, Beccles, Suffolk.*

Contents

Acknowledgements

My thanks are due to many colleagues in the trade union movement, especially in the General and Municipal Workers Union, and, in particular, to my principal and research assistants in the GMWU Pensions and Social Services Department, Myles J. White and Sue Ward. Their advice, assistance, and encouragement were invaluable during the research and writing of this book.

I must also acknowledge the constructive attitudes of the many companies and their managements with whom I have been involved in negotiations on pension schemes, especially British Leyland, Guest Keen & Nettlefolds, and Pilkington who kindly permitted summaries of their pension negotiations to appear in these pages.

I must thank my wife, Eileen, for her considerable secretarial assistance and encouragement, particularly as the writing of this book coincides with the busiest time ever for those engaged in pensions in the United Kingdom.

Finally, I would emphasise that any errors or omissions within this book are my responsibility alone.

HARRY LUCAS

Introduction

Due to fundamental differences in approach, the main political parties have taken the best part of two decades to develop a bipartisan approach to pensions in the United Kingdom. The Labour Government's Social Security Pensions Act 1975 is due to come into force in April 1978 and the Conservative Party in opposition has pledged, should it be returned to power, not to change the basis of the new State scheme. This long-awaited foundation must be built upon. A partnership between State and occupational pension schemes is envisaged to produce the concerted effort necessary to tackle the unacceptable spectre of poverty in old age.

No one can be proud of the fact that 2 million pensioners at present exist solely because of State supplementary benefits. That perhaps a further million pensioners do not claim such benefits due either to ignorance of their entitlements or, it is suggested, to the supposed stigma of claiming these rights.

On the other hand, occupational schemes have developed to the extent of some 65,000 schemes embracing a membership in excess of 11 million full-time employees. Taxation advantages, employers seeking to retain competitiveness of employment conditions, the "hard sell", and latterly the powerful influence of the trade unions have all contributed to the dramatic increase in schemes and membership during the last 20 years.

The growth in occupational schemes, with particular emphasis in the non-manual sections of employment in the private sector and throughout the public sector, has produced a hotch-potch of anomalies and, regrettably yet understandably, considerable envy.

Suspicions, not all unfounded, have abounded on the part of those who have been denied membership or access to schemes. Bewilderment abounds, too, on the part of management and employees when confounded by the jargon that enshrouds pensions in a mystique of its own. Harmful to an otherwise beneficial aspect of industrial relations have been the barriers often purposely erected around numerous schemes, thus preventing members understanding the problems of pensions management and, in many instances, denying employees the basic right of knowing their entitlements and benefits. The latest and proposed legislation concerning pensions and scheme membership—with the welcome introduction of member representative trustees, is opening up the pensions scheme to thousands for the first time. This book will therefore provide a guide for all who are charged with the responsibility of obtaining a working knowledge of pensions and an understanding of the powerful swing of pensions into the field of collective bargaining.

Pensions and Industrial Relations, because of the authorship, is written from a trade union viewpoint, and as such has been designed to assist representatives of unions and management when participating in consultations and whenever pensions are subject to collective bargaining.

A multiplicity of subjects spanning the pensions spectrum are included and make essential reading to anyone directly or indirectly involved in negotiating and administering pension schemes.

Trustees, representing members or from management, and members of pensions committees can acquaint themselves with the various facets of the pensions scene *up to April 1978 and well beyond.*

It is no idle statement to say that pensions *must* be the "bridge" upon which to improve industrial relationships.

CHAPTER 1

The Development of Pensions in Britain

THE STATE

There are examples of pension provision dating back well over 300 years, but it is only over the last 30 years or so that pensions have become a significant feature of the pay package. Over the same period successive governments have become increasingly involved with national pension schemes.

Though not the first statute to deal with relief of destitution, the Poor Relief Act 1601 can be regarded as the starting point of State provision for social security.

It was not until 1908, however, that the first real departure from the Poor Law occurred with the introduction of the Old Age Pensions Act. Despite the pensions provided being small and subject to a means test, this legislation represented new thinking on the part of the Government of the day.

Social change was still to be a low priority, with no further progress made until 1925 when the Widows' and Orphans' and Old Age Contributory Pensions Act introduced the first national scheme of contributory pensions.

OCCUPATIONAL PENSIONS

A century earlier, in May 1825, Charles Lamb published an essay which he called *Superannuated Man* dealing with the subject of his own retirement. He was only 50 at the time and received a pension of two-thirds of his salary after 33 years of service. From this account it would appear there has been a marked lack of progress in the field of retirement provision since then. The essayist's pension was an *ex gratia* one, so perhaps it may be assumed that it was on an exceptionally favourable basis. Nevertheless, it does illustrate a long history of providing earnings-related pensions.

Shortly after, in 1829, a formal pension scheme for the Metropolitan Police was established, to be followed in 1834 by the Civil Service scheme. These were, of course, schemes for public servants. In the private sector the history of occupational schemes is much more recent, less widespread, and, in the main, far less generous (see Appendixes I and II for the distribution and membership and non-membership of occupational schemes).

In the years leading up to the Second World War, following the introduction of the Income Tax Acts of 1918 and 1921, there was a significant increase in the number of private and occupational schemes, indicating no fundamental change in government policy, but there were several minor developments in the coverage and benefits of State pension provision throughout the same period.

BEVERIDGE COMMITTEE, 1942

In 1942 a committee headed by Sir William Beveridge reported on the future of social insurance and the allied services. The report recommended an extensive development of the social insurance services to include provision against want due to sickness, disablement, and old age. Also established was a "minimum subsistence level" in respect of all these categories, maintaining that the State should provide, as of right, pensions which were adequate without recourse to other means.

WELFARE STATE—LABOUR GOVERNMENT, 1945–51

The Beveridge Report formed the basis for pension provision under the Welfare State introduced by the 1945–51 Labour

Government. It has remained the line of established Trades Union Congress and Labour Party policy. This emphasis on State pension has not deterred various Labour governments from introducing legislation aimed at facilitating the improvement and extension of occupational schemes.

NATIONAL INSURANCE ACT 1959 (THE BOYD-CARPENTER PLAN)

The next major change in national pension policy came with the Graduated State Pension Scheme introduced by a Conservative Government. The Graduated Scheme started in April 1961, benefits and contributions being related to earnings, initially in excess of £9 per week, to supplement the State flat rate pension. Known as the Boyd-Carpenter Plan it was considered as wholly unsatisfactory by reason of the evidence of the redistributive element of any pay-as-you-go social security system. Successive governments failed to communicate successfully to contributors, who were disenchanted with the graduated pension secured by their graduated contributions and upon learning that part of their contributions was to provide other Social Insurance benefits. The Scheme was terminated in April 1975 with all accrued benefits frozen at that date and payable together with other pensions at State pension age.

NATIONAL SUPERANNUATION AND SOCIAL INSURANCE BILL 1969 (THE CROSSMAN PLAN)

The Labour Government in 1969 introduced a comprehensive bill to provide earnings-related State pensions from earnings-related contributions with a pension entitlement of a higher percentage of earnings for the lower paid worker than for the higher paid. Pensions were to be based on the current money value of pensioners' earnings at retirement, and generous provision was to be made for those retiring before their new scheme contributions entitled them to the full benefits. An equal deal for women pensioners was also proposed, and there was to have been preservation of pension rights for a member leaving the membership of an occupational scheme. The Crossman Plan, as it came to be known, would have merged flat-rate and earnings-related State benefits into a single scheme with somewhat complicated contracting-out provisions for employers with occupational schemes. The proposals, however, did not become law as they were rejected by the Conservative Government elected in 1970.

SOCIAL SECURITY ACT 1973 (THE JOSEPH PLAN)

The incoming Government published their own long-term proposals on pensions in September 1971 in a White Paper called *Strategy for Pensions* which was subsequently given legislative effect as the Social Security Act 1973. The Act laid greater emphasis on private occupational schemes than would have been the case under the Crossman Plan. It was the essence of the Act that a basic flat-rate scheme with benefit levels similar to those at present would be supplemented by membership of "recognised" occupational schemes. The "recognition tests" represented minimum standards which private schemes would have to provide to be "recognised" as a legally acceptable alternative to a State Reserve Scheme.

The Reserve Scheme was intended to provide a second pension for employees not fortunate enough to be in better occupational schemes. It was to be on a "money purchase" basis, the inadequacy of which became even more obvious during the subsequent unanticipated inflation at a rate not previously experienced in this country.

THE AWAKENING OF THE TRADE UNION MOVEMENT'S INTEREST IN PENSIONS

It was the Conservative Government's Counter Inflation [Temporary Provisions] Act 1972 *and* their intended State Reserve

Scheme which triggered off the grand awakening of the trade union movement's interest in pensions. Up to that time the manual unions had given the wage packet and other terms and conditions of employment their priority consideration: partly due to historical reasons—the endless battle to obtain improvement in their members' basic earnings in seeking parity with white collar earnings; partly due to the members themselves continuing to press for immediate financial advantage with taxation and the cost of living being the barriers to an increased standard of living; partly due to the vast majority of employers refusing to negotiate on pensions, particularly for non-staff employees.

The second stage of the Programme for Controlling Inflation—the name given to their Pay Code by the Conservative Government—specifically excluded improvements in pensions from the pay limits, providing a direct incentive for the trade unions to negotiate pensions at the same time as negotiating restricted pay increases—an incentive which was acted upon with alacrity by the forward-looking unions with the co-operation of some employers.

Some unions were slow off the mark on this pay exemption, but they quickly joined the ranks of their thrusting colleagues who by then were committed to the task of ensuring that their members were not to be consigned into either the State Reserve Scheme or an occupational scheme merely meeting the "recognition" requirements. The unions regarded the State Reserve Scheme as being aptly named and unacceptable, and they acted accordingly.

The General and Municipal Workers Union at their 1973 Congress clearly recognised that its officers and members should take a much greater interest in the occupational pensions movement and confirmed that the Union had a duty to prevent members from being "consigned" to the wholly unsatisfactory State Reserve Scheme. In pursuit of these objectives the GMWU established at national level a specialist department to deal with pensions and social security matters, responsible for advising and training officials and lay representatives negotiating in this area. A giant union had stepped into the pensions arena.

However, it was not the unions that stopped the introduction of the Reserve Scheme. The Labour Government which took office in February 1974 announced the abandonment of the State Reserve Scheme in the following May and promised a White Paper containing new pension proposals.

ABANDONMENT OF THE STATE RESERVE SCHEME

Little or no useful purpose could be served in discussing all the rights and wrongs of the abandonment decision—it is now but history. Reaction at the time varied from full support to outright rejection of the decision, even among the major unions. The delay in starting the second State pension is regrettable—although with hindsight one can perceive that earlier implementation would have but aggravated the subsequent general economic situation. *Nevertheless, sooner, rather than later, a solution has to be found to the problem of providing an adequate level of pensions without recourse to supplementary benefits for those retiring in the next decade.*

No one produced information on those employers who could have afforded to improve an existing scheme or implemented a new scheme between the abandonment of the State Reserve Scheme (May 1974) and the implementation of the Castle Plan (April 1978). Not all employers will ever find the will, or the way, of introducing a new scheme or improving an existing one without a statutory spur (some employers will always welcome the readymade reason for delay, and they were to be pleased again a year later with the pension improvements surprisingly included in the Government's 1975 "attack on inflation" package—from which developed the Social Contract with the TUC). Wrangling on the Reserve Scheme abandonment decision rumbled on, but later the GMWU were able to state that between May 1974 and November 1975 the Union had been actively involved in negotiating the inauguration of 112 new or improved schemes covering between 1¼ and 1½ million workers. All had *not* been lost—conclusively, pensions had been brought into collective bargaining.

THE LABOUR GOVERNMENT'S BETTER PENSIONS PLAN, 1975 (THE CASTLE PLAN)

In September 1974 when the White Paper was published, Mrs. Barbara Castle, the Secretary of State for Social Services, said: "I have called this White Paper 'Better Pensions' because that is precisely what our proposals will achieve. Our policy in pensions is to secure better benefits for all pensioners, present and future: those in occupational schemes and those without cover." The Social Security Pensions Act 1975 received the Royal Assent on 7 August 1975 and will become effective from 6 April 1978.

Chapter 2 is devoted to the Act, contracting-out considerations and its most important aspect—the requirement placed upon employers with occupational schemes to consult with the trade unions whether or not they seek to contract out.

THE OCCUPATIONAL PENSIONS BOARD (OPB)

Under the Social Security Act of 1973 a new body was established —the Occupational Pensions Board. Originally the main responsibilities given to the Board were:

(i)   To issue "recognition" certificates to employers with schemes which fulfilled the requirements to exempt them from the State Reserve Scheme which was to have commenced in April 1975.

(ii) To supervise the financial arrangements of recognised schemes to ensure that benefits up to the recognition level had proper financial backing (both these functions were ended with the abandonment of the Reserve Scheme in May 1974).

(iii) To decide whether the rules of schemes conformed with the requirements for preservation of benefits for members who left before normal retirement age.

(iv) To assist in the modification of the rules of schemes or their winding up, for specified purposes, where those concerned did not possess the necessary powers or where scheme procedures were unduly complex or cumbersome.

(v)   To advise the Secretary of State on proposals to make regulations under the Act which affected occupational pension schemes.

(vi) To advise the Secretary of State, when asked, on general questions affecting pension schemes (reports subsequently published by the OPB include those on Member Participation, Disclosure of Information, Equal Status, and Solvency).

The Social Security Pensions Act 1975 added to the OPB's responsibility the granting of certificates for contracting out to occupational schemes that meet the required standard from April 1978. Furthermore, the OPB now has wide powers of supervision of a fund's assets, investment operation, and portfolio in those cases where a contracting-out certificate is issued.

The OPB has a strong working link with and occupies the same building as the Superannuation Funds Office (Apex Tower, New Malden, Surrey KT3 4DN: telephone 01-942 8949). The joint offices issue memoranda to clarify procedure, documentation, and generally to assist those inaugurating or amending schemes in preparation for approval or contracting out. These memoranda are issued from time to time as statutory instruments, legislation, or experience make it appropriate.

The task of the OPB is a formidable one, charged as it is in the main to protect the interests of prospective pensioners' deferred pay.

The previous imbalance between representatives on the Board from the pensions movement as compared with those from the trade union movement was partially corrected by new appointments made to the Board in October 1976.

THE PENSIONS PARTNERSHIP

Several factors, including inflation and undoubtedly politicians, will determine the development of the partnership envisaged by the

Castle Plan—the partnership between State and occupational pension schemes. The majority of opinions on all sides is that for the foreseeable future the State will be hard pushed to provide pensions for everyone at subsistence level. Such are the demands and pressures on the Social Services benefits that pensions will almost certainly remain a political football, until, that is, a government grasps the nettle of establishing the priorities with those best suited to represent the views of the working populace. The first priority must surely be to provide higher State pensions for those who are already retired or will retire with little or no additional provision from the Castle scheme and have no other source of retirement income. Further improvements in the State scheme and the lowering of the pension age must be planned, costed, and the cost paid.

Within any industry or any company the partnership must be "measured" in one of two ways:

EITHER   the totality of benefits to be provided for the workforce by the State (adjusted from time to time) *plus* an occupational scheme, e.g. a total pension of 80–85% of final earnings after 35 or 40 years of service;

OR   the totality of the costs to be shared between employer and employees for the State *plus* an occupational scheme, e.g. total contributions to the State's Social Insurance and to the occupational scheme of 35–40% of payroll.

Whichever approach is used a satisfactory solution can only be achieved by negotiation. *The successful launching or amendment of major schemes over recent times has been dependent upon the trade unions being in a position to endorse acceptance by their membership.*

OCCUPATIONAL PENSIONS AS PART OF TOTAL REMUNERATION

For employees to obtain the maximum benefit from existing and proposed occupational pension schemes there must be an acceptance of pensions as part of the total remuneration package and central to collective bargaining. Certainly up to the time that there was a general acceptance of pensions being *deferred pay*, the trade union movement was suspicious of the introduction of misleadingly described "fringe benefits". The advantages of obtaining wage settlements were never in doubt as against pensions over which there existed such limited control and participation. Legislation should have removed any doubts.

(Chapter 6 discusses the objectives and realities in pension negotiations.)

RELUCTANT EMPLOYERS

There is a marked reluctance on the part of those employers who adopt a paternalistic approach towards pension provision—comparable with the gold-watch-for-40-years-of-faithful-service approach. Despite the advances in industrial relations being skilfully improved, pensions have all too often figured as "perks"—a reward for loyal staff employees yet a privilege to be earned by manual workers. This attitude has caused many employers to hold an entirely misplaced view on the rightful place of pensions. The "cake" to be apportioned on the table of negotiation must include provision for existing and prospective pensioners. Effective use of the Employment Protection Act 1975 by all independent trade unions can bring that about.

PENSIONS AND INFLATION

The State Pension Scheme in Britain, both pre- and post-1978, in keeping with most other State schemes throughout the world, is not funded. Benefits are paid out of income by direct or indirect taxation; those at work are providing for those in retirement.

Pay as you go is the apt description of the unfunded scheme. Perhaps its greatest disadvantage is that benefits already promised may be increased either intentionally or unexpectedly on account of inflation without adequate increases to current contributions. Will future contributors always be financially able, let alone willing, to meet the costs? In times of high inflation the additional burden of increased benefits in money terms is merely passing on a blank cheque for the next generation to complete—and pay.

Pensions schemes on the pay-as-you-go system are unacceptable to employees in the private sector; pensions are deferred pay and the workforce entitled to them cannot afford the risk of loss should the employer go out of business for whatever reason.

The impact of inflation upon funded schemes presents other problems. Apart from some exceptions in the public sector, it is customary for occupational pension schemes to be funded. A fund is built up of the contributions paid by the employer and, if contributory, by the employees. The fund is invested and accumulated with interest from which benefits are paid, and unless paid separately by the employer the cost of administration is also met by the fund.

The rate of contributions to a pension fund is based on recommendations made by an actuary. In calculating the contribution rates for the benefits to be provided the actuary requires:

(a) details of the total work force eligible for the scheme divided between males and females;
(b) the wage/salary rates and structure (both present and to be anticipated);
(c) the turnover of labour normally experienced;
(d) the incidence of early retirements due to ill health, redundancy, or a member's own request;

together with any other information relevant to the particular group of employees such as particularly hazardous occupations.

Actuarial knowledge adds the readily available mortality and expense factors and provides the professional expertise needed to decide upon the prospective interest yields and wage increases—both of which depend upon the assumption to be made on future inflation.

This particular aspect of pensions can perhaps best be summarised in a quotation from a consulting actuary's report (similarly worded comment is to be found in the reports of most actuaries that have been made during and since the period that inflation outstripped investment yield):

"If in the long run, pension funds are unable as a result of political or economic influences to earn a return which matches inflation, there is not much financial sense in funding final salary pension schemes. They may well be continued because of the additional security offered by the separation of the pension assets from the Employer, but unless adequate returns can be achieved, some employers (and unfortunately probably the weaker ones) may come to feel that the price is too high."

COMMENT

If the rate of inflation is not drastically reduced and brought under control, it will be obvious—and this is the point made by the actuarial profession—the cost of providing pension schemes could become insupportable. At that stage being reached the nation's entire economic structure is brought into question and the entire approach to pensions would, of necessity, be subject to considerable amendment. In the meantime I support the view that before such an unprecedented state (in the United Kingdom) is reached, the cost of providing pensions would most likely be more difficult to maintain without a fund.

Any attempt to abandon funding *prematurely* would be resisted in no uncertain terms by pension-scheme members and their representatives. The supporters of such a course of action surely cannot appreciate the disastrous consequences of wrecking excellent relationships that have been carefully nurtured by the unions between management and workforce in the field of pensions. Even if economic circumstances destroy the financial case for funding pensions, the objective of security for the employee's benefit, independent of his employer's undertaking, remains a strong argument for funding.

CHAPTER 2

The Social Security Pensions Act 1975
—Contracting In or Out—
The Consultation Process

A CONSOLIDATING ACT

The Social Security Act 1975 is a consolidating Act which brings together the divergent strands of social insurance law previously found in the National Insurance Acts, the Social Security Act 1973, and other minor Social Insurance legislation. It retains the new system of wage-related National Insurance contributions and tidies up the administration of the National Insurance system. As a consequence a great mass of statutory regulations have been up-dated and re-issued. For the foreseeable future claimants will continue to qualify for and receive short-term benefits, such as sickness and unemployment benefit, in much the same way as they have been accustomed to.

The Social Security Pensions Act 1975 provides that retirement pensions and certain other benefits shall be earnings-related; it introduces a two-tier retirement pension plan and specifies the terms on which good occupational pension schemes may be partially contracted out of the new State plan after consultation with the trade unions. The Act requires that men and women shall be given equal access to membership of occupational pension schemes (note that the requirement is equal access to membership—not equal benefits). The Act makes other changes to social insurance law, the most notable being the abolition of the married women's option to contribute at the reduced rate. The option was abolished in April 1977 but there will be transitional arrangements to safeguard the position of working wives and widows who have previously elected to exercise the option. Unemployment and sickness benefit will be paid at the same rate to men and women irrespective of marital status and, with the abolition of the "half-test", it should be easier for married women to qualify for a retirement pension in their own right. The Act also provides for the introduction of a new non-contributory mobility allowance for the severely disabled.

The greater part of the Pensions Act is devoted to the new retirement pension plan and the arrangements for enabling good occupational pension schemes to contract out of the State plan and coexist in partnership with it.

The new State plan will commence on 6 April 1978. The basis of the new structure will be a lower earnings limit and basic component, and an upper earnings limit and additional component.

Contributions will be related to the earnings limits and retirement pensions, and other earnings-related benefits will be related to the basic and additional components.

Since April 1975 Social Insurance contributions have been deducted in the same way as PAYE income tax. Expressed in current terms (April 1977), in any week that an employee earns £15.00 (lower earnings limit) Social Insurance contributions are payable on all earnings up to £105 (upper earnings limit). The upper earnings limit is about equal to one and a half times the national average wage at the time it was fixed.

The contribution rates for the Castle Plan 1978 will depend upon a number of factors, one of which is the number of workers contracted out of the State scheme. In his calculations the Government Actuary has assumed that 8 million employees will be contracted out. This figure includes 4 million employees in the public sector. The precise contributions will be fixed nearer April 1978, but illustrated contributions for those contracted into the State scheme are 10% for employers and 6½% for employees of all earnings up to the upper earnings limit—a total contribution of 16½%. This compares with a total of 14½% (8¾% employers, 5¾% employees) applicable from April 1977 on all earnings up to £105.

Employers' contributions were increased by a further 2% from April 1977 by way of a pay-roll tax; the additional revenue did not go to the National Insurance Fund.

The Castle Plan 1978 will retain the new system of earnings-related contributions. The lower earnings limit will be fixed each April and will be approximately equal to the current rate of the basic retirement pension for a single person. They will not necessarily be identical because regulations provide for rounding off of the earnings limits (in April 1977 terms: lower earnings limit £15; basic component £15.30).

The upper earnings limit will be approximately seven times the lower earnings limit. Again, in order to facilitate rounding off, in practice it may be fractionally more or less than seven times in any one year.

RETIREMENT PENSIONS

The Act introduces the two-pension structure consisting of two components:

(1) The basic component is the basic flat-rate State pension (the "Old Age" pension). Only the name has changed.
(2) An additional component which is related to earnings within a specified band (see below).

The basic component will be the minimum retirement entitlement of all contributors who satisfy the contribution conditions. As we have seen, its monetary value will be very close to the lower earnings limit but not necessarily identical (in April 1977 terms: lower earnings limit £15.00; basic component £15.30).

The additional component will be related to all earnings between the lower and upper earnings limits—in April 1977 terms £15 and £105. Initially the additional component pension will accrue at 1 ¼ % or 1/80th of earnings within the upper band for each year between 1978 and 1998. Thereafter it will be expressed as 1 ¼% of the average of the best 20 years' earnings in a contributor's working life from April 1978. Such earnings will be revalued to reflect any decline in purchasing power between the years they were earned and the year before State retirement age.

Such retirement age remains 65 for men and 60 for women.

Using April 1977 rates only for the purpose of illustration, a person entering the State scheme on 6 April 1978 at 45 years of age (male) or 40 (female) and contributing at the maximum rate will calculate his or her retirement pension as follows:

(1) Subtract the lower earnings limit from the upper earnings limit. £105 minus £15 = £90.
(2) 20 years at 1 ¼ % per year = 25%.
(3) 25% of £90 = £22.50—the additional component.
(4) Add the basic component of £15.30 to give a total personal pension = £37.80.
(5) To which must be added the adult dependant's allowance—£9.20 in the case of married men whose wives depend on their husband's contribution record—£37.80 plus £9.20 = £47.00 for a married couple.

For those employees who contribute to the new State scheme for more than 20 years, "pensionable" earnings will be the average of the best 20 years' revalued earnings; such years need not be consecutive. The pension will then consist of an additional component of 25% of average earnings revalued, a basic component, and the adult dependant's allowance in appropriate cases.

A married woman who is employed and has contributed on earnings above the lower earnings limit will be entitled to a basic component and an earnings-related additional component in her own right.

If a married couple both qualify for a pension each in their own right and have both retired when one dies, the survivor will inherit the pension of the deceased. This is on the assumption that the resulting total pension does not exceed that which could have been earned by a person who had consistently paid contributions at the maximum rate.

Widows with dependent children or who are expecting a child by their late husband at the time of his death and widows who are 50 years of age or over at the time of their husband's death, or when their children cease to be dependent, will receive an additional component equivalent to the whole of their husband's additional component entitlement at the time of his death.

Women who are widowed or who cease to be entitled to a widowed mother's allowance between ages 40 and 50 will be entitled to a proportion of their late husband's additional component at the date of his death. The proportion of the pension to which she will be entitled is determined by reducing the total pension by 7% for each year or part of a year by which her age is less than 50 at the time of her husband's death or when she ceased to be entitled to a widowed mother's allowance.

A woman who becomes a widow before she is 40 who has no dependent children will not be entitled to a widow's pension.

Widowers' invalidity pensions will be payable if the husband is a long-term invalid and incapable of work at the time of his wife's death and his late wife satisfied the contribution conditions.

INVALIDITY BENEFIT

The Castle Plan provides for early retirement to a modest extent. The flat-rate invalidity pension will be replaced by an earnings-related pension, calculated in exactly the same way as the new two-tier retirement pension. The allowance will be paid in addition to the pension but conditions for payment of the upper rates will be eased.

Widows who are incapable of work due to long-term ill health when their husbands die or when they cease to be entitled to a widowed mother's allowance will be entitled to an invalidity pension provided they are either not entitled to a widow's pension or are entitled to a widow's pension at a reduced rate.

MARRIED WOMEN'S OPTION

At present married women and most widows enjoy the option to pay contributions at a reduced rate of 2% of all earnings up to the upper earnings limit. Contributions at this rate do not qualify the contributor for sickness, unemployment, or retirement benefits, but the right to industrial injury benefits is retained.

The Social Security Pensions Act provides that as from April 1977 the option is to be brought to an end. Married women and widows entering employment after that date will have to pay contributions at the full rate. Women in employment at that date who have chosen to pay contributions at the reduced rate will be permitted to retain the option. If, for any reason, they cease to be employed for two full tax years, on their return to work they will be liable to pay full contributions.

Unemployment and sickness benefit will be paid to men and women at the same rate, irrespective of marital status, if the claimant satisfies the contribution conditions. With the abolition of the half-test and the introduction of the average-of-the-best-20-years-revalued-earnings rule, it will be easier for working wives to qualify for retirement benefit in their own right.

EQUAL ACCESS

Following the general trend of current legislation against discrimination on grounds of sex, the Social Security Pensions Act requires that the rules of occupational pension schemes must be drafted so as to enable men and women to join the scheme on the same terms regarding the age of admission, length of service needed to become a member, and whether membership is voluntary or a condition of service.

An occupational pension scheme is any scheme or arrangement comprised in a trust deed or similar legal instrument which relates to any job category or description and which is capable of having the effect of providing benefits in the event of death or retirement, in pension form or otherwise, for workers or their dependants or personal representatives. It makes no difference whether a scheme is contracted out of the State scheme or not, or whether it is a scheme designed to ride on top of the State scheme providing additional benefits over and above the State scheme benefits on a contributory or non-contributory basis.

It will still be possible to discriminate by category of employment —to have a staff scheme without making provision for manual workers—but it will be unlawful to discriminate only on grounds of sex. The practice of having schemes which are open to male employees only or are obligatory for males but voluntary for females, or with different lower age limits and periods of qualifying service will be unlawful after April 1978.

Where scheme rules are changed either to provide that women are to be admitted to the scheme or to make membership of a scheme obligatory where it had previously been voluntary, existing employees who are not members of the pension scheme will retain the right to decide whether to become members.

Where, after 6 April 1978, it is shown there has been a breach of the equal access rules, the employer may be required to fund past-service benefits for the employees concerned for a period of up to 2 years without contribution by the employees or any other member of the scheme.

PROTECTION AGAINST INFLATION

All long-term benefits in payment will be increased periodically to protect them against erosion by inflation. Both components of retirement benefit will increase. The basic component or flat-rate pension will be increased in line with the growth in national average wage or prices, whichever is the more advantageous to pensioners. The additional component or earnings-related second-tier pension will be increased by reference to the level of price increases. The additional component of other long-term benefits, such as widows' benefits and invalidity pensions, will also be increased in line with prices.

CONTRACTING OUT

Good occupational pension schemes will be able to contract out of the State scheme and coexist in partnership with it. Contracted-out schemes must satisfy minimum standards or tests in order to qualify for a contracting-out certificate. A certificate will be issued by the Occupational Pensions Board at the request or "election" of an employer after consultation with the trade unions. The relevant regulations are contained in SI 1975 No. 1927, and paragraph 4(3) provides that any question whether an employer has complied with the requirements as to consultation may be referred by the employer or by a trade union to a tribunal.

In effect contracting out is partial and consists of transferring the responsibility for providing an additional component or earnings-related retirement benefit from the State scheme to the contracted-out scheme.

The Social Security Pensions Act adds a system of earnings-related retirement, invalidity, and widows' benefits to the existing benefit structure of the Social Security Act 1975. Members of contracted-out occupational pension schemes will still have to pay social security contributions but at a lesser rate on earnings above the lower earnings limit. It is anticipated that the joint contracted-in contribution will be in the order of 16½% of earnings up to upper earnings limit. The joint contribution will be reduced by 7% of earnings above the lower earnings limit (employer 4½%, employee 2½%), if contracted out.

The tests that occupational schemes must meet to be contracted out are:

(1) The requisite benefit test (also known as the "quality test").
(2) The guaranteed minimum pension test (also known as the "quantity test").

REQUISITE BENEFITS

Only a final salary or average salary revalued scheme will qualify for contracting out of the State scheme.

If the pension is to be calculated on average annual salary, the method of doing so must be approved by the Occupational Pensions Board. In general the OPB will expect the average to be reached by dividing the total pensionable earnings by the number of years of pensionable service in the contracted-out scheme. In making this calculation pensionable, earnings in each tax year must be revalued by the same percentage ordered by the Secretary of State for Health and Social Services to apply for the purpose of revaluing earnings in the calculation of the State pension.

Final salary schemes will normally be approved by the OPB if they use any of the following definitions:

(1) Average annual salary of the best 3 years in the last 13 years of service.

(2) The average annual salary of the last 3 years of service.

(3) The salary in the last year of service.

(4) The salary for the best year in the last 3 years of service.

Whichever formula is adopted the resulting pension rights must accrue at a minimum of 1 ¼ % or 1/80th of final salary or revalued average salary for each year of contracted-out pensionable service.

The OPB has discretion to approve an accrual rate lower than 1 ¼ %, provided the Board is satisfied that the lower accrual rate will provide benefits which as a whole will not be less favourable than the requisite benefits. For instance, if a scheme provided a pension and a lump-sum retirement allowance, the scheme will be approved if the total of the pension and the pension value of the lump sum are equivalent to an accrual rate of 1 ¼ % for each year of contracted-out service.

THE GUARANTEED MINIMUM PENSION

Scheme rules must provide that members will be assured of a guaranteed minimum pension. The guaranteed minimum pension will be calculated by the Department of Health and Social Services.

In broad terms the GMP is equivalent to the pension the member would be entitled to had he been a member of the State scheme throughout his period of contracted-out service.

In addition to the member's requisite benefit and GMP, schemes must provide a requisite benefit and a GMP for widows. If a pension scheme member dies either in service or after retirement leaving a widow, she must be given a pension calculated at an annual rate of at least ⅝% of the member's annual average salary or final salary. In short, a pension equivalent to at least half the deceased's requisite benefit.

The widow's GMP is half the GMP to which the member was entitled when he died including any increase that may have been due because the deceased had postponed retirement. In addition to her scheme benefits a widow will be entitled to the widow's benefit provided by the Social Security Act 1975 as amended by the Social Security Pensions Act 1975. Her title to such benefit will be determined according to her age and family circumstances.

EARLY LEAVERS

The Social Security Act 1973 required that the rules of occupational pension schemes be altered to ensure that scheme members who leave service before retirement date shall be entitled to a deferred pension provided they have attained 26 years of age and completed 5 years' pensionable service. The preservation rules came into effect on 6 April 1975; pensionable service before and after that date counts in the computation of the 5-year period of qualifying service.

The Castle Plan 1978 retains the preservation rules and imposes the additional obligation for contracted-out schemes that the deferred GMP shall be revalued to protect its value against erosion by inflation. Any one of three methods of revaluation may be adopted:

(1) The preserved GMP may be revalued by reference to the revaluation orders issued by the Secretary of State for Health

and Social Services for the revaluation of earnings for purposes of the State scheme.

(2) Occupational pension schemes may limit the obligation to revalue deferred GMPs to 5% per annum compound or in line with the Secretary of State's revaluation orders, whichever is the lower. If this method is adopted the employer must pay a single limited revaluation premium to the State scheme.

(3) As an alternative to limited revaluation, schemes may provide that deferred GMPs be revalued at a fixed annual rate, which has been initially set at $8\frac{1}{2}\%$ per annum. If this method is adopted there is no requirement to pay a limited revaluation premium but the anual rate of $8\frac{1}{2}\%$ is fixed without the alternative to apply the rate of the Secretary of State's revaluation order should this be less than $8\frac{1}{2}\%$.

In the event of a scheme member leaving contracted-out pensionable service before having completed 5 years' membership in the contracted-out scheme and without qualifying for a deferred pension under the 1973 Act rules, the member's accrued GMP must be preserved. Alternatively, the employer may pay a contributions equivalent premium to the State scheme in order to extinguish the member's right to a GMP and the contingent entitlement to a widow's GMP.

A contributions equivalent premium is a single payment representing the difference between the reduced contributions paid during contracted-out service and the contributions which would have been paid to the State scheme if the employees concerned had not been contracted out. The effect of such a payment will be to "buy" back the member into the State scheme.

The GMP and the contingent widow's GMP becoming the equivalent of the pension a contracted-out employee would receive from the State scheme had he not been contracted out, provision is made to ensure that it really is guaranteed. It must not be a paper promise; it must be secured by a trust deed, a policy of insurance, or an annuity contract. Before the Occupational Pensions Board can issue a contracting-out certificate they must be satisfied that the resources of the scheme are sufficient to meet the priority liabilities including the GMP. Once the certificate is issued and remains current the OPB will continue to supervise the solvency of schemes and the employer will be required to submit documents and information relating to the solvency of the pension fund and the security of GMPs and other priority liabilities. In the event of the resources of a scheme being considered insufficient the OPB may order the employer to make payments to the scheme. Should the employer fail to do so the OPB may make a further order declaring the amount outstanding to be a debt owed to the Board. They may then recover the debt and transfer it to the pension fund. Debts to occupational pension funds in respect of members' and employers' contributions are to be included in those debts given priority in the event of bankruptcy.

RESPONSIBILITY FOR CONTRACTING OUT

All employees without exception will have to "join" the State scheme unless they are excluded because they are members of a contracted-out occupational pension scheme.

The responsibility for deciding whether to contract out of the State scheme in respect of any group or category of employees rests with the employer. In the language of the Act and regulations, the employer is required to make an election". In making an election the employer is not permitted to discriminate between different employees who are members of the company scheme on any grounds other than the nature of their employment, the most obvious example being that it would be lawful to elect to apply for a contracting-out certificate in respect of "staff" employees as a whole, or the "hourly-paid", or "foremen and supervisors" as a whole.

Once having decided the category or categories of employments to contract out the employer may not subdivide the categories with a view to excluding a particular group—say women. The only exception to this rule is that employees who are unable to complete 5 years' contracted-out pensionable service may be excluded from the contracting-out certificate.

Where there is an existing or prospective occupational pension scheme, the employer is required to give at least 3 months' written notice of his intention to the employees concerned. This includes those employees, if any, who are not to be contracted out. Written notice must also be given to other interested parties and to any independent trade union recognised to any extent for the purpose of collective bargaining which represents employees who are scheme members. The employer is also required to enter into consultation with the trade unions.

Two practical points need emphasis:

(1) Written notice of intention must be served on any independent trade union recognised to any extent for the purposes of collective bargaining. There is no direction as to whom the notice should actually be delivered.

(2) Consultation is not defined, but if the consultation between employers and unions is to mean anything, both sides should jointly examine and discuss the financial and industrial relations implications of the decision whether or not to contract out, with a willingness to arrive at a mutually acceptable solution through a genuine interchange of views and information.

THE PROCEDURE FOR CONTRACTING OUT

(i) NOTICE OF INTENTION

The groups to whom the employer must give notice are:

(a) those who would be contracted out;

(b) those who would be contracted out except that they would retire at normal pension age with less than 5 years' membership;

(c) those who are in employments to be covered by the election but who are not scheme members;

(d)   those who are scheme members but are in employments the
      employer does not intend to contract out;

i.e. notice must be given to all scheme members plus those who would
come under the new contracted-out scheme. It does not have to be
given to groups whom the employer has always refused to admit and
does not intend to admit now (e.g. manual workers in a staff scheme).

However, under the contracting-out regulations, schemes can only
discriminate in terms of the nature of an individual's or group's
employment, so where a scheme has formerly excluded women doing
the same jobs as men, it must now give them notice of the intention to
contract out.

The notice should be given to employees:

(a)   by sending or delivering it in writing to each of them; or
(b)   by exhibiting it conspicuously at the place of work or employ-
      ment and drawing each employee's attention to it in writing;
      or
(c)   "in such other manner as the Occupational Pensions Board
      may consider reasonable in the circumstances of the case."

It should also be given in writing to all independent trade unions
recognised to any extent for the purpose of collective bargaining in
relation to the employees concerned. (It is not stated at what level
within the union it should be given. It will be for both officials and
stewards to ensure that all those likely to be in contact with the
company receive a copy of the notice.)

The notice must at least cover or explain the following items in a
way that those reading it can understand:

- Name of scheme.
- Employments to be contracted out and the effective date.
- Benefits to be provided by the scheme.
- Effect of contracting out on State scheme benefits and contri-
  butions.
- Changes to be made to scheme benefits.
- Date of expiry of notice and address for inquiries and repre-
  sentation.

- Right of employees and independent trade unions to make representations direct to the OPB.

Experience has shown that many companies shroud their pension schemes in mystery and their notices or letters about them only make things more confusing. It will be important to ensure that the notices fulfil the requirement of being in a form that those reading them can understand, i.e. simple, clear language, and a minimum of jargon. Where there is a substantial non-English-speaking group among the employees, a translation should at least be available.

(ii) CONSULTATION

After giving these notices, the employer is required to undertake consultations with all independent trade unions recognised to any extent for the purposes of collective bargaining in relation to the employees concerned. As the notices need to be given at least 3 months before the contracting-out date, it is obviously better if consultations can in fact start before that date (and include the form of the notice).

The approach to the consultation process must be practical, realistic, and attuned to the needs of particular groups of workers. It must not be overlooked that a pension scheme is to be planned and funded until the youngest contributor dies in retirement.

The employer or the trade unions have the right to refer to an industrial tribunal the following questions:

(a) whether an organisation is an independent trade union;
(b) whether the union is recognised to any extent for the purposes of collective bargaining in relation to the employees concerned;
(c) whether the employer has complied with the consultation requirements.

Item (a) will effectively be decided by the certification officer, whose decision is binding on the tribunal. Item (b) should be regarded as a question of fact which the tribunal will determine on the evidence of any agreement reached or of any negotiations about such agreements.

The question of whether an employer has complied with the requirements of the regulations as to consultation will be a question of fact to be determined by the industrial tribunal on the evidence before it.

APPLICATION FOR CERTIFICATE

When the notice has expired and the consultations are complete, the employer can then "make his election" (i.e. apply for a certificate of contracted-out status) to the OPB. He must do this within 3 months after the notice has expired or start the whole procedure again.

Together with the application, the employer must submit the following documents or give a satisfactory explanation of their absence:

(a) a copy of the notice given to employees and to any appropriate trade union;

(b) a copy of the trust deed and rules except where these are already held by the Joint Office of the OPB and Superannuation Funds Office;

(c) an actuarial certificate that the resources of the scheme are sufficient to pay out the benefits promised;

(d) for an insured scheme, a copy of the insurance contract if it forms the basis of the rules of the scheme.

When the OPB has received the application ("election" in technical terms) the Board has to be satisfied that the correct procedure has been followed. It will consider representations at this point, either on the procedure or on the question of discrimination.

Provided the proper procedure has been followed, the rules of the scheme are satisfactory (i.e. they satisfy the minimum contracting-out conditions and only discriminate in terms of the nature of employment) and the financial provision is adequate, the contracting-out certificate will be issued.

SCHEMES COVERING MORE THAN ONE EMPLOYER

Many of the larger pension schemes are run by group holding companies to cover all the individual companies or divisions within their group. In this case, the holding company can be treated as the employer for purposes of consultation provided that all the unions concerned have agreed in writing to this arrangement.

But where there is a federated scheme covering an industry or part of one, where the member employers are not in business association with each other, each employer will be responsible for carrying through the procedure himself.

Some employers have two schemes for the same employees, i.e. life assurance and pensions are legally separate schemes. They will be allowed to treat these as a single scheme but they must make it clear in all notices.

The OPB are entitled to review their decision to grant a certificate on any grounds within 6 months of the decision or longer at their discretion. At any time they can review it if they are satisfied that there has been a relevant change in circumstances or that there was originally a material mistake in fact. They can review it either on their own initiative or on the application of an interested party (which would include an appropriate union).

NOTICE OF DECISION NOT TO CONTRACT OUT

The procedure where an employer with a pension scheme decides not to contract out is similar, and so need not be covered at such length. The employer who has, or intends to establish, a pension scheme in force on 5 April 1978 must give notice of his decision before 7 December 1977. For schemes established after that date, at least 3 months' notice must be given.

This notice must be given to the following employees:

(a)   those who are members of the scheme;

(b) those who are in the same employment as scheme members but are not themselves members (e.g. those who are too young or have not worked for the company long enough to be members).

Notice must also be given to the trade unions.

The details that must be covered in this notice are:

(a) the changes, if any, it is intended to make in scheme benefits and/or contributions as a result of not being contracted out;
(b) the additional earnings-related benefits payable from the State scheme as a result of not contracting out and the contributions which are payable;
(c) the persons to whom representations can be made.

The employer must then undertake consultations in exactly the same way as an employer intending to contract out. But as it is a negative decision there is no requirement to submit documents to the OPB and there are no sanctions to be applied. A proposal not to contract out is equally important and must be taken as seriously as a proposal to contract out.

THE CONSULTATION PROCEDURE

In most cases the view can be taken that consultation should take place through the normal negotiating channels. However, where there is a multi-plant company where negotiation is normally done at plant or industry level, it may well be necessary to request the setting up of company-wide machinery on this pensions issue. It is not usually possible to have a company pension scheme which differs from plant to plant; common discussions and a common view are therefore essential.

It is important, wherever practicable, to ensure that a strong element of shop-steward representation is involved in the consultation exercise. Stewards are normally in the best position to know the feelings and circumstances of their members at shop-floor level.

It is equally important to ensure that the company's own industrial relations or personnel experts are involved.

MAKING THE DECISION

I regard the choice as not being between contracting in and contracting out, but between either:

(A) contracting in with a "ride-on-top" scheme in addition; or

(B) contracting out with a scheme structured to provide benefits substantially better than the minimum level necessary to contract out.

Choice A   A "ride-on-top" scheme is one that provides the benefits that the State scheme does not provide, either with the employer paying the full cost or with the employee making some contribution. For example, the GMWU model "ride-on-top" scheme, which has been successfully negotiated on a non-contributory basis, includes the following benefits:

(a) Lump sum on retirement of up to one and a half times final pay for 40 years' service.

(b) Lump-sum payment on early retirement on grounds of ill health or any other grounds when over age 55.

(c) Insurance against death or permanent total disability whilst in service—one and a half times the previous tax year's PAYE earnings.

(d) The scheme is administered by a 50/50 committee of management and unions.

The above should be regarded as the minimum range of benefits to be provided in a scheme to "ride on top" of full participation in the State scheme.

It is possible to add a pension formula to augment the State's provisions but there is no simple approach to harmonising the two on a basis fair to all members of such a scheme. Account has to be taken of the level of benefits already promised under an occupational scheme. The modification of existing expectations would present not only administrative difficulties but potential harm to industrial relations.

The pensions industry is divided in its opinions on the subject of providing the partnership between State and occupational schemes on a totally integrated basis. Pensions, from both sources, have to be measured on the grounds of fairness, adequacy, and the feasibility of total understanding by the potential beneficiaries. I have strong doubts if a formula based on total integration would measure up to other than the adequacy "test".

Choice B   By contracting out with a scheme offering benefits well in excess of the minimum requirement it can obviously be demonstrated that the objectives of the unions and their members are being met—fair, adequate, and understandable.

In financial terms alone there is no incentive to contract out with a "bare bones" scheme, i.e. one that meets minimum contracting-out requirements. It is equally true to say that such an approach will bring no appreciation from the unions who would be failing their members if the opportunity was not taken of shading consultation over into negotiation.

FACTORS TO BE TAKEN INTO ACCOUNT

1.   INDUSTRIAL RELATIONS CONSIDERATIONS

Whilst the State scheme remains on a pay-as-you-go basis the need for complementary funded occupational schemes is paramount. The great majority of members of occupational schemes understand and value the security of a fund kept apart from their employers' accounts. There has been a general awakening to the fact that pension funds provide the capital and generate the income upon which much of industry survives. Strong doubt has been thrown on the correctness of the channelling of some pension fund resources—there are increasing demands to harness and direct investment power to rejuvenate industry, to secure jobs, and in part to meet social objectives. There is a simple but logical sequence in the thoughts of the majority of workers not to rely solely upon the State for retirement provisions and to accept the principle of "deferred pay" being funded. From that base it is but a short step to seek contracting out (together with member participation) in order to obtain or retain the control and flexibility which is unavailable under the State scheme.

It must also be borne very much in mind that the entrenched trade union view of "what we have we hold" is incompatible with any suggestion to replace membership of an occupational scheme by full participation in the State scheme.

Given adequate information by means of a good communication exercise, employees will agree that under current legislation contributions to an occupational scheme rank for tax relief; furthermore, that there is a reduction in the total Social Insurance contribution when contracted out. A suggested way of illustrating this feature is included in Chapter 4 on Communications.

2.   FINANCIAL CONSIDERATIONS

The reduction in Social Insurance contributions of 7% (2½% for members and 4½% for employers) of earnings between the lower and upper earnings limits is the main financial consideration to contracting out. It is necessary for the calculation to be made to establish whether the guaranteed minimum pension costs more or less than this 7% in order to determine if contracting out represents a cost or a saving.

The Government Actuary calculated the 7% reduction as being the amount necessary to meet the cost of the GMP based on assumptions including age and earnings distributions. It was also assumed that there would be a real return of investments of ½%, i.e. the gap between investment yield and wage inflation.

Any group of employees whose ages and wages compare favourably with the Government Actuary's assumptions naturally produce costings in close keeping. A preponderance of women producing an earnings distribution greatly different from the ratio between men and women used by the Government Actuary tips the scales significantly against contracting out.

The most vital financial consideration, however, is the assumption to be made on the yield gap, the real return on investments. If one holds the opinion that the recent experience of a negative real return on investment will continue, then funded schemes—let alone contracting out—will go by the board. Should future wage increases not be held in check and, coincidentally, interest rates fall, it will not only be funded schemes that will disappear.

I support the optimistic view that inflation will be brought under effective control and that a real rate of return on investments can be assumed in the longer term. Given the appropriate circumstances, and they can vary tremendously from employer to employer, then a contracting-out decision can be recommended. A "blanket" decision of "in" or "out" is inappropriate—only a close examination in each case of the facts and figures can guide the proper decision.

In view of the degree of judgement involved in reaching the decision it is important to note that to contract in or out is not an irrevocable decision. The option for a scheme to cease to be contracted out and to buy back in total into the State scheme will be available at any time. Such action would have to be weighed very carefully against possible industrial relationship consequences at the time.

3. ADMINISTRATIVE CONSIDERATIONS

The consultation requirements, the need to meet the GMP, and the treatment of early leavers have all been discussed. The contracted-out scheme will also be subject to controls not previously applied. Annual statements from trustees, administrators, auditors, or insurers will be required by the Occupational Pensions Board in confirmation that contributions have been paid. The OPB will also require a regular actuarial certificate at about 3-year intervals. This will certify that GMP liability is fully covered by assets if the scheme were to be wound up and the rate of funding required to maintain that position. The OPB has power if not satisfied to insist on increased contributions, or any deficiency to be met by the employer. It would be a mistaken view to consider that contracting out is the easy option.

4. POLITICAL CONSIDERATIONS

The Labour Government made clear in their *Better Pensions* White Paper and reiterated during the passage of the Bill through Parliament, so skilfully handled by the late and lamented Brian O'Malley (then Minister of State for Social Services), that they expected the new State scheme to operate in partnership with well-founded occupational schemes. The major trade unions have endorsed this philosophy by their constructive attitude in the consultation process. It should not, however, be taken to imply that the unions would accept a contracting-out decision at no matter what cost to their members.

In Opposition, the Conservative Party has unequivocally stated, both in and outside the House of Commons, that upon being returned to Government they would not alter the basis of the Pensions Act. The Liberal Party welcomed the Act's provisions.

As far as can be reasonably assessed, therefore, the Castle Plan is to be the basis upon which pensions will develop in the United Kingdom for the remainder of this century.

COMMENT

I believe that we are at the make or break point of occupational pension schemes. If the statutory consultation is mis-handled or we get overtaken in procedural wrangles before the OPB or industrial tribunals, not only will irreparable harm be done to members' occupational pension expectations, but industrial relationships may be disturbed in a way that will take much invaluable time to mend.

Consultation between employers and unions must lead to a joint consideration of all the problems raised by the contracting-out issue with a view to arriving at a *joint* decision in the interest of all the employees concerned.

It is clear that the OPB would not issue a contracting-out certificate while the question of the adequacy of the consultation procedure was being considered by an industrial tribunal. If subsequently the issue is settled, then the OPB may, under Regulation 8(2)(d) of the Certification of Employments Regulations, specify an earlier date from which it will have effect, i.e. the contracting-out certificate may be back-dated.

If this situation arises, then State scheme contributions from the effective date of the certificate will have been at the wrong rate, as the employer and employees will have paid at the full, not contracted-out rate until the certificate was actually issued. In the event the employer, by following the procedure set out in the *Employers' Guide to National Insurance Contributions*, Leaflet NP 15, will be able to refund any over-deduction to the employee, correct the earlier entries on the deduction card, and adjust his next payment to the Collector of Taxes.

Whilst the procedure does allow for correcting the situation, the possible industrial relations consequences of members paying contributions to an occupational scheme (suitable for contracting out) and the full, not contracted-out rate to the State should dissuade most employers from attempting to conduct inadequate consultations with the unions.

CHAPTER 3

Planning and Designing Pension Schemes within the Limitations and Requirements of Legislation

So that the employer and employees can obtain tax relief in respect of contributions to a pension scheme, the benefits are required to conform to certain rules based partly on legislation and partly on practice. Over the years successive pieces of pension legislation had produced a hotch potch, one of the main disadvantages of which was that different rules had to be complied with depending on which piece of legislation the scheme was approved under.

By the Finance Act 1970 a "new code" of approval was set up designed, in theory, to simplify matters. All new schemes since April 1973 have been required to conform to this new code and all schemes in existence before that date (now called "old code" schemes) will be required to conform to the new code by April 1980. If before 1980 they are amended in any material way, they must conform to the new code immediately they are amended. Most of the rules relating to the new code are set out in a booklet issued by the Inland Revenue Superannuation Funds Office entitled *Occupational Pension Schemes— Notes on approval under the Finance Act 1970 as amended by the Finance Act 1971*, but universally called the Practice Notes (see the summary of current legislation as it concerns pension schemes at the end of this chapter).

The main methods of providing pensions are:

Firstly, by money purchase—where the annual payment is related to earnings each year and the emerging benefits are of uncertain amount. The State Reserve Scheme—the part of the Social Security Act 1973 which was abandoned by the Labour Government in May 1974—is an example of this type of scheme. A variant on a pension based on fixed contributions is the pension which is fixed in relation to each year of service so that each employee's pension is directly related to his period of pensionable service but not to his earnings. This type of scheme, until comparatively recently, was common for hourly paid employees.

Secondly, by average salary scheme—under which a pension of fixed amount is provided in respect of each year of pensionable service but that fixed amount is related to earnings in the year in question. This type of scheme was developed during the inter-war years and used extensively over a long period. Provided the unit of pension per £ of earnings was reasonable it produced a pension which was reasonable irrespective of the employee's earnings pattern, but only if there was no inflation. Its other attraction was that it produced a relatively stable cost year by year.

Thirdly, by final salary scheme—the central feature of a pension scheme is the member's own pension, not least because its form and amount will influence other benefits, particularly dependant's benefits. It is appropriate therefore to develop the explanation of a scheme's structure from this base element. The explanation that follows embraces all the features of a final salary scheme, including the definition of "final salary" itself.

THE MEMBER'S PENSION

There are three important factors to be determined in arriving at the calculation of the member's pension:

(1) The earnings pattern—do earnings, ignoring the effects of inflation, start at a low level and increase throughout the working life as in the case of most salaried employees, or do they alternatively rise to a peak in middle life and decline in

the years immediately before retirement, as is the case with some heavy manual workers?

(2) Inflation—the aim should be to provide a pension directly and reasonably related to income during the member's working life. The impact of roaring inflation will be appreciated by all—if not fully understood. An informed judgement on future inflation has to be taken into account in determining the bases for the calculation and cost of pension.

(3) Length of service—the length of service with an employer should influence the amount of pension entitlement, otherwise there will be understandable friction between long-serving and short-serving employees.

Reverting to the earnings pattern, this can lead to the development of two fairly different types of scheme, both taking account of the other two factors.

The member on a salary which increases throughout his career will seek a pension related to his earnings immediately before retirement, the conventional final salary scheme under which the pension is a fraction of his salary at or just before retirement multiplied by the number of years of pensionable service being entirely acceptable. Pensions calculated in this manner automatically take account of inflation *during* the working lifetime.

The formula described in the previous paragraph does not meet the needs of a member whose earnings, ignoring inflation, had reached a peak 10 years or more before retirement and declined steadily since then. The definition of "final salary" permitted by the Inland Revenue, to be discussed later, will not normally enable the earnings in the best years to be counted. Consideration in such circumstances must be given to the average salary scheme where the earnings over the whole period of pensionable service count towards the pension.

As already stated, the efficiency of the average salary scheme has been impaired by the effects of inflation, hence the development of the average salary *revalued* scheme.

In this instance, the earnings in each separate year of pensionable service are revalued in line with the increase in the cost of living during the period from when the money was earned until normal retirement date. The member will then receive a pension which in purchasing power is related to the purchasing power of his average earnings during his working life, and the effects of inflation are nullified.

In February 1974 the Inland Revenue announced that they would allow the calculation of final remuneration, for pension purposes, by increasing the past average earnings by a factor to allow for inflation. The Revenue stated then that this was intended for employees who step down or whose earning power is reduced, or for those whose earnings had been restricted under the previous counter-inflation policy. Nearly 2 years later a new memorandum stated that: "such evidence as is available to the Superannuation Funds Office suggests that dynamised final remuneration is being used mainly to justify larger benefits for highly paid executives and directors, and is not being limited to employees whose earnings in real terms have fallen because of a reduction in status or earning capacity."

With the new State scheme adopting a variant of the average salary formula, clearly the unions, employers, and the Inland Revenue Superannuation Funds Office will have to revise their ideas to bring the average salary revalued formula in wider use than it was in the past.

"SERVICE" AND "SALARY"

Passing now to the consideration of such words as "service" and "salary" and their alternative definitions:

1.   "Service", clearly, means the period of a person's employment with an employer, whereas "pensionable service" normally means the part of the total period of service which counts for pension purposes. Ideally, the two should be the same. However, problems can occur:

   (i)   *At the start of a new scheme with employees having varying periods of service before the scheme commences.* Service is divided into past service and future service. Regrettably more often than not no pension rights are granted (a) in respect of such past service, (b) in respect of only a portion of it, or alternatively granted (c) at a lower rate than rights in respect of future service. If no distinction is made between past and future service—the objective of all unions—the two added together become pensionable service.

(ii)   *When employees are required to satisfy a qualifying period before being eligible to join the scheme.* Once served, however, qualifying service can and should be regarded as pensionable.

As stated already, ideally all service should be treated as pensionable service, although this can cause problems being created under the legislation relating to preservation of pensions on withdrawal, to which later reference is made.

For the purposes of definition, service whilst an employee is a member of a scheme is often referred to as "scheme service".

2.   In relation to pensions when using the word "salary", it is really remuneration that is being described, whether it be salary, wages, or some other basis such as commission or bonus earnings: in particular, the remuneration which is used for the purposes of calculating benefits and contributions under the scheme—what is called "scheme salary" or "pensionable salary". There are almost limitless possibilities because different trades and occupations are remunerated in many different ways. The following are the more usual emoluments which can form part of scheme salary:

(a)   Basic annual salary.

(b)   Annual equivalent of basic weekly wage.

(c)   Annual equivalent of a basic hourly rate of pay for a standard working week.

(d)   Fluctuating emoluments such as commission, overtime, and bonuses. The Inland Revenue normally require fluctuating emoluments to be averaged over a period of at least 3 years.

(e)   Gross PAYE earnings during an income tax year.

As a result of the increase in the Social Security pension it has increasingly become the practice in calculating scheme salary to make a deduction from pensionable pay to take account of the State pension. Alternatively, the actual pension calculated in accordance with the pensionable earnings is reduced by the State pension or part of it.

With the introduction of the new State scheme, which in itself is a system of integration because of its two-tier structure, no doubt many new and interesting methods of integrating benefits under State and occupational schemes will be devised.

Integration, or as it is sometimes called "harmonisation", will continue to be the subject of considerable controversy between management and the unions and their members. However, it must be appreciated that as the cost both to employees and employers of providing the State pension increases, the argument in support of some measure of integration has to be considered. It may be that in order to ensure the survival of good occupational schemes the unions will have to concede some measure of integration, while reserving their right to negotiate the most effective formula for the particular company or industry workforce.

Scheme salary is usually calculated on each scheme anniversary (mostly but not always the anniversary of the commencing date) and remains unchanged for all purposes of the scheme during the next 12 months irrespective of what happens to actual remuneration during that period.

The next factor to consider is "final salary" (or terminal pensionable salary or a number of other phrases meaning the same), and this is where the scheme planner becomes involved with Inland Revenue requirements as set out in the Practice Notes.

In these notes it is stated that terminal salary may be computed on one of the following bases:

(i) remuneration (i.e. scheme salary) for any one of the 5 years preceding the normal retirement date; or

(ii) the average of total emoluments for any three or more consecutive years ending not earlier than 10 years before normal retirement date (effectively 13 years).

Variations on these bases are possible and the most common variation is that scheme salary (which may be basic emoluments or a mixture of basic and average fluctuating emoluments) is itself averaged over a period of years.

If final salary is pay during a year other than that ending at normal retirement date, or is an average of three or more years' earnings, each year's earnings may be increased in proportion to the cost of living for the period from the end of the year up to normal retirement date.

It should be noted that even where no averaging is required, emoluments must be taken over a period of at least 12 months. This is to prevent the possibility of an employee being granted a large increase in salary on the last scheme anniversary before retirement (which may be only a few days before retirement) and the increased salary being treated as final salary. In these circumstances the last scheme salary which could be used would be that during the last *complete* scheme year before retirement, but increases in the prices index during the period from the end of the year until retirement could be applied.

CALCULATION OF PENSION

All the factors which come into the calculation of the pension except the actual fraction of final salary (or average salary) which is earned by each year of service have now been considered.

There is a need here to refer to the Practice Notes because the question of maximum pensions has to be heeded. There are two main facts for guidance:

(i)   The pension must not exceed a maximum of two-thirds of final remuneration (which need not be final salary calculated according to the rules of the scheme but may be some higher figures calculated in one of the ways permitted by the Inland Revenue). This maximum applies to all benefits from the current employment (including the pension equivalent of non-pension benefits such as tax-free lump sums) plus, in certain circumstances, benefits retained from previous employment.

(ii) The standard fraction which will be approved without query is 1/60th of final remuneration for each year of pensionable service provided this latter does not exceed 40 years at normal retirement date.

If, therefore, the fraction does not exceed 1/60th and the pensionable service cannot exceed 40 years at normal retirement date, no problems can arise with the Revenue. Moreover, if there are no other benefits from the current employment but there are retained benefits from a previous employment, these retained benefits may be payable even if, when added to the benefits from the current employment, the total pension is in excess of two-thirds of final remuneration.

It is permissible to provide a fraction in excess of 60ths so long as the potential service to normal retirement date is at least 10 years and the total pension cannot exceed two-thirds of final remuneration.

If potential service is less than 10 years the two-thirds maximum must be progressively scaled down so that if potential service is 5 years or less only the standard 60th is permitted for each year.

INFLATION PROTECTION

The final salary type of scheme has come to be the most widely used scheme because it is the type which in most cases provides the highest pension and thus the greatest measure of protection against inflation up to the time of retirement. Then comes the problem of inflation while the pension is in course of payment. For many years schemes for public servants and some of the larger privately funded schemes have made a practice of increasing pensions in course of payment from time to time but generally not in accordance with any predetermined plan. Among insured schemes the practice was very rare until the early 1970s.

Continuing inflation has focused attention on the post-retirement inflation problem and now, whatever the type of scheme, inflation protection is possible, and an increasing number of schemes provide it. It takes one of three forms:

(a) discretionary increases from time to time;
(b) increases in line with increases in the cost of living—Pensions (Increase) Act 1971;
(c) increases at a fixed rate such as 3% or 5% per annum.

Whatever the method used, where the pension exceeds the maximum which would have been approved at normal retirement date, further increases must not exceed the greater of 3% per annum compound and the increase in the cost of living, which is usually measured by the Index of Retail Prices.

There are some fairly complicated rules about funding in advance for such increases which are further complicated by the effect of commuting part of the pension at retirement.

COMMUTATION

The ability of a retiring employee to commute part of his or her pension for a tax-free lump sum has long been a valued benefit. Where commutation is permitted under an old code scheme the commutable part is usually limited to one-quarter of the member's pension so that the cash payment varies with the size of the member's pension. In certain types of old code scheme the whole pension can be commuted and it has always been possible to commute the whole pension if its amount is trivial—£39 per annum under the old code— or if the retiring employee is in exceptionally serious ill health. Under the old code, commutation of a trivial pension under a section 379 scheme gave rise to a liability on the trustees for income tax at the rate of one-quarter of the standard rate.

Under the new code of Inland Revenue approval the commutation is not directly related to the pension—it is the lump sum itself which is controlled by the Revenue. The standard lump sum (equivalent to the 60ths pension) is 3/80ths of final salary for each year of pensionable service up to a maximum of 40 years. This gives a maximum lump sum of 120/80ths, i.e. one and a half times final salary.

As in the case of the 60ths pension it is possible to provide a fraction greater than 3/80ths provided the maximum of 120/80ths is not exceeded, but the difference is that scaling down of the maximum is required when service is less than 20 years (not 10 years as for the pension) and the standard 3/80ths only is permitted if service does not exceed 8 years.

Because the cash is regarded as a retirement benefit it is necessary to convert it into equivalent pension to ensure that together with the non-commutable pension it does not provide a pension exceeding the two-thirds maximum. The Revenue have indicated a basis for the conversion and for males retiring at age 65 with a pension payable for at least 5 years, whether or not the pensioner survives that period, there has been virtually universally adopted a formula of £1 of pension being equivalent to £9 of cash. There are other formulae for different ages and types of pension and for females but they tend to differ slightly from scheme to scheme.

Another feature of the new code which is different from the old code is that a lump sum within the limits laid down may be provided even though there is no pension. Hence the development of the "cash benefit only" type of scheme in conjunction with contracting in to the State scheme.

Full commutation of a pension for triviality (£52 per annum under the new code) or in exceptionally serious ill health is permitted as under the old code, but if the lump sum exceeds the maximum permissible, tax at a rate of 10% is payable on the excess.

NORMAL RETIREMENT DATE

Having considered most of the points arising in connection with the employee's pension if retirement takes place at normal retirement date, one must also consider what happens if he retires earlier or later. But first an explanation of what is meant by normal retirement date.

Under the State scheme a man becomes entitled to his pension on the date when he attains age 65 and a woman, on her own insurance record, at the date when she attains age 60, and these are the normal retirement dates under the vast majority of occupational schemes. (It is worthy of note that to meet the TUC's objective of lowering the State pension age for men to 60, the latest figures estimated by the DHSS reveal a first-year cost of £2000 million.)

However, the Revenue will permit a normal retirement date which is the date of attainment of any age within the range of 60–70 for men or 55–65 for women. Ages outside these limits will be considered in special circumstances and, in particular, an earlier retirement may be permitted where earlier retirement is the custom because of the nature of the occupation.

EARLY RETIREMENT

A scheme member is permitted to retire with an immediate pension provided age 50 has been attained, but there is no necessary age qualification for early retirement on grounds of incapacity.

If the retirement is due to incapacity the member may be provided with a pension of the same fraction of final remuneration as would have been received had service continued up to normal retirement date. Final remuneration would be calculated as if the actual date of retirement were the normal retirement date.

"Incapacity" means, according to the Revenue Practice Notes, physical or mental deterioration which is sufficiently severe to prevent the member from following normal employment or which may seriously impair earning capacity: it does not mean simply a decline in energy or ability.

If retirement is not due to incapacity a 60ths pension is permissible for the years actually served or, if the amount would be greater, a pension calculated as if the retirement were due to incapacity but reduced by a factor N/NS, where N is the actual service and NS is the potential service to normal retirement date.

This is the maximum pension allowable. In practice it is not uncommon for the pension earned by service to date of retirement to be reduced by ½% for each month by which the actual retirement date precedes the normal retirement date.

The lump-sum cash payment on early retirement is calculated on broadly the same basis as the early retirement pension and differs depending on whether or not incapacity is the reason for the premature retirement.

LATE RETIREMENT

An employee who remains in service after normal retirement date may be granted additional pension up to the maximum approvable on the basis that the actual date of retirement is the normal retirement date, i.e. two-thirds of final remuneration, or a lesser amount if actual service is less than 10 years.

If the total actual service exceeds 40 years, each year in excess of 40 served after normal retirement date may earn an extra 60th up to a maximum of 45/60ths of final remuneration.

As an alternative the pension at normal retirement may be increased actuarially to reflect its later commencement, and in fact late retirement pensions in many schemes are calculated in this manner, giving an increase of rather more than ½% for each month that retirement is deferred.

Lump-sum cash payments may be similarly increased but the rate of increase will be lower.

Even though employment continues after normal retirement date it is permissible for the pension and/or the lump sum to be paid immediately.

DEPENDANTS' BENEFITS

So much then for the benefits for the employee. What benefits are to be provided under the modern scheme for his dependants if they survive him? These take two main forms:

(a) a lump sum payable if he dies in service;
(b) a pension to dependants whether death occurs in service or after retirement.

(a) LUMP SUM DEATH BENEFIT

Under the new code the *maximum* lump sum permitted on death-in-service is the greater of £5000 and four times final remuneration.

Final remuneration in this context is usually the scheme salary at the date of death, but where scheme salary assumes a deduction to take account of the State pension it is usual for this deduction to be ignored on the theory that there is no State death benefit equivalent to the State pension.

In addition to this lump sum, the deceased member's contributions to the scheme may be refunded with or without interest.

(b) DEPENDANT'S PENSION

(i) *DEATH IN SERVICE* In addition to the lump sum death benefit there may be payable a pension to the surviving widow or widower or other dependant. The *maximum* single pension is two-thirds the maximum pension which could have been paid to the deceased member had he retired owing to incapacity on the day he died. If, however, there is more than one pension, i.e. a pension for the surviving spouse *and* a pension for one or more dependants, the pensions in total must not exceed the whole of the member's incapacity pension and no single pension may exceed the two-thirds limit, but within these limits any division is permissible.

Dependant means a person who is financially dependent on the employee or was so dependent when he died, but a child is always regarded as dependent until he attains the age of 18 or ceases to receive full-time educational or vocational training if later. A pension for a child must cease when the child ceases to be dependent.

A very common level of widow's pension is 50% of the member's incapacity pension (i.e. a pension based on the member's remuneration at death but on his total potential service to normal retirement date) and it often continues until the youngest child ceases to be dependent instead of there being separate pensions for dependent children. Widowers' pensions as of right are, as yet, rare, although in practice many schemes do in fact, on a discretionary basis, pay pensions on cases of proven financial dependency. The unions certainly are pressing for all such pensions to be dependants' pensions, not restricted to widows, for example.

Incidentally, all lump sums and pensions from the same employment must be aggregated for the purposes of the maximum approvable, and in certain circumstances similar benefits from previous employment must also be aggregated.

(ii) *DEATH IN RETIREMENT*   When death occurs after retirement, dependants' pensions may be payable calculated in the same manner as if death had occurred in service but are related to the maximum pension which could have been paid to the member when he retired even though this maximum pension was not paid to him. It is becoming common practice for a 50% widow's pension to be incorporated as of right, although some schemes are only meeting guaranteed minimum pension requirements, i.e. based on the member's service from April 1978 onwards.

In addition to a pension provided in this way as a distinct benefit under the scheme, the employee may at retirement surrender part of his or her own pension to provide a pension payable to a dependant and commencing on the member's death, but the pension so provided must not exceed the reduced pension payable to the member. This type of dependant's pension was, until comparatively recently, the only dependant's pension provided under many schemes.

Inflation proofing of dependants' pensions is permitted in the same manner as inflation proofing of the member's own pension.

Where the pension is payable if death occurs after retirement, the inflation proofing may commence from the date the member's pension commences, not from the date of death.

WITHDRAWAL FROM SERVICE

Having considered what happens if the employee remains a member of the scheme until he dies or retires, there is one other major event which may occur—he may leave the service of the employer either voluntarily or on dismissal either for redundancy or for some other reason.

In the past, the rules of schemes have usually provided that if an employee was dismissed for redundancy he was entitled to benefits secured by both his own and the employer's contributions, but if he left for any other reason he was entitled only to the benefits secured by his own contributions. Whatever the scheme rules provided, in the vast majority of cases an employee took a refund of his contributions whatever the reason for leaving, and the Revenue's rules were that if such a refund was taken the employee was not entitled to any benefit from the employer's contributions.

The practical effect of this was that the employee who changed jobs several times during his career, and each time took a refund of his contributions to the pension scheme, was entitled at retirement only to the pension provided under the scheme of his last employer, which was usually comparatively small because the period of service with that employer was short.

This pattern is much more likely to be found among staff employees than manual workers. A manual worker who leaves pensionable employment and takes a return of contributions is more likely to find himself dependent on the State pension in retirement.

The part of the Social Security Act 1973 relating to the preservation of pension rights which came into force in April 1975 is designed to prevent this situation occurring. The preservation provisions of the 1973 Act are simple in concept but difficult in application.

The general principle is that members of an occupational pension scheme who leave their job voluntarily or otherwise before normal retirement date, who have completed the necessary qualifying service and who are not retiring early, shall be entitled to have their accrued pension rights preserved for them until they reach normal retirement age, but provision may be made to pay the preserved benefit earlier if the member subsequently retires before normal pension age on grounds of ill health. Early leavers must not be treated less favourably for any purpose relating to scheme benefits than they would be treated if they remained in employment to normal pension age. The benefits with which we are concerned are those benefits to which the member would become entitled at normal retirement age, normal retirement age for this purpose being the age specified by the scheme rules.

Entitlement to benefits on leaving service is not established directly by the Act but must derive from the rules of each pension scheme. There is not therefore a statutory right to preserved benefits but there is a statutory requirement that pension schemes shall provide such benefits and that scheme rules shall be amended to comply with this requirement.

The statutory requirements outlined here are minimum requirements. There is nothing to prevent an occupational pension scheme from providing better terms, say deferred pensions after one year's service or dispensing with the age qualification.

The preservation rules are to be found in Section 63 and Schedule 16 of the Social Security Act 1973. They came into effect on 6 April 1975.

To explain the rules as simply as possible it is preferable to deal with them in two stages:

(1)   The position after 6 April 1975 up to April 1980.
(2)   The position after April 1980.

THE POSITION AFTER 6 APRIL 1975
UP TO APRIL 1980

An employee who, on leaving service, has less than 5 years of pensionable service or has not reached 26 years of age is entitled to a return of his own contributions and the occupational pension scheme has no further obligation towards him. Alternatively, the scheme may offer a deferred pension or a transfer of the member's pension rights to another scheme, but there is no statutory obligation to provide anything other than a return of the member's contributions.

An employee who, on leaving service, has attained age 26 years *and* has completed 5 years of pensionable service is entitled to a deferred pension, that is a pension calculated on the basis of his earnings at the time of leaving, taking account of service performed and "frozen" until normal retirement date. In addition to the pension, any other benefit the member would have enjoyed *had he remained in service to normal retirement date*, such as a pension for his widow if he dies after retirement, must also be preserved.

There is no obligation to preserve the benefit of any improvement to the pension scheme effected *after* the member ceased to be employed by the sponsoring company.

The obligation imposed on pension schemes by the 1973 Act is to preserve short-service benefits for early leavers who qualify. Schemes are *permitted* to offer a return of contributions or a transfer of pension rights or an annuity contract as an optional alternative to preservation. There is no obligation to include any of the alternatives —the obligation is to provide a deferred or "frozen" pension. In practice most schemes offer one or more of the alternatives. As we shall see, the option of a return of contributions is to be limited still further.

In calculating the 5-year period of pensionable service account is to be taken of pensionable service *before* 6 April 1975 as well as after. The service need not be continuous, just so long as it all ranks for pension and in the aggregate adds up to 5 years or more. It need not relate to a single occupational scheme. It may be that the employer has terminated one pension scheme in order to replace it with a better one—the service in both schemes is qualifying service; similarly, on promotion an employee may have transferred from the works scheme to the staff scheme; again the service in both schemes is all qualifying service. If there is a waiting period before an employee is admitted to the scheme, provided the employee enters the scheme automatically and becomes entitled to benefits in respect of the waiting period without any further action on his part, then the waiting period counts as qualifying service for preservation purposes.

THE POSITION AFTER APRIL 1980

As from April 1980 a scheme member who satisfies the qualifying conditions on leaving service will be entitled to preserved benefits as previously described, but in respect of pensionable service after 6 April 1975 the member will not be able to opt for a return of his own contributions. Scheme rules may provide the option of a return of contributions in respect of service before 6 April 1975, but benefits accrued after that date *must* be preserved.

If for any reason a member is deprived of the option to take a refund of his contributions the scheme must ensure that that member's preserved benefits are increased by at least 3% per year compound. Alternatively, the trustees must be satisfied that the benefits "exceed or compare reasonably with" the amount of the member's contributions. It is normal for scheme rules to contain this latter provision without any reference to escalation.

The most common reason why some pension fund members are prevented from opting for a return of contributions is the application of the Inland Revenue rule to the effect that the option may not be allowed to members whose earnings have *in any year,* while they were members of the scheme, exceeded £5000.

The Social Security Pensions Act 1975 adds a new dimension to contracted-out schemes because it provides that deferred retirement benefits to the equivalent of the guaranteed minimum pension must be increased by a guaranteed predetermined percentage per annum compound according to which formula is adopted.

Furthermore, as the GMP must be preserved for anyone who by the 1973 rules qualifies for a deferred pension under a contracted-out scheme—no matter what alternatives may be contained in the scheme rules—the practical effect will be to bring the 1980 restrictions forward by 2 years.

The 1973 Act does not contain requirements about the records to be kept by scheme administrators to ensure that preserved benefits are paid; nor does it require any particular form of document to be given to early leavers. Administrators are left to devise their own procedures for making sure that they can, as far as possible, establish contact with members when their preserved benefits become due and for making sure that members or their dependants are aware of the procedures for claiming benefit and for notifying any change in their circumstances.

Generally speaking, schemes must not contain rules to deprive a member of entitlement to preserved benefits should he fail to notify a change in circumstances, e.g. marriage, or he or his dependants fail to claim benefits when they fall due. With rare exceptions members may not be deprived of deferred benefits because they were dismissed for fraud or misconduct.

Nothing in the 1973 Act excludes the operation of the Limitation Acts, and in any event the 1973 Act allows that in the event of a claim for deferred benefits being made 6 years or more after the benefits become due, arrears of benefit relating to the period which ended 6 years before the claim was made need not be maintained.

The Occupational Pensions Board is the body charged with the task of interpreting and supervising the preservation rules. It also has a broader advisory role and will now supervise the contracting-out procedures under the Social Security Pensions Act.

CONTRIBUTIONS

For many years there has been a continuous debate as to whether it is better for the benefits under a scheme to be provided entirely at the expense of the employer or whether the employees should also contribute. The unions prefer non-contributory schemes but suffice it to say that nowadays in the majority of schemes employees are required to contribute and this raises the question of the method by which such contributions are calculated.

In a scheme where benefits are earnings-related the member's contribution will normally also be earnings-related. It will be a percentage of scheme salary and will remain unchanged during each scheme year. It must not exceed a maximum of 15% of remuneration.

All members' contributions to new code schemes are allowed as a deduction from income in assessing liability to tax. Under some old code schemes, however, members' contributions are treated for tax purposes as if they were life assurance premiums.

ELIGIBILITY

There are three main ways in which the entry to an occupational scheme can be restricted:

(a) by class of employee, e.g. staff but not works;
(b) by age, e.g. over age 18 but under age 64 males and 59 females;
(c) by service, e.g. after completion of 12 months of service.

In the past, entry to a scheme has often been severely restricted by the use of one or more of these devices, but such restrictions are gradually easing.

Certainly in the future it will not be possible to discriminate against women in this area, but works employees are still, over a wide field, treated differently from staff employees, and even if the eligibility conditions are the same the level of benefit is often different.

As to age limits, it is now quite common to admit the whole age range from, say, age 18 or 21 to normal retirement age.

On the grounds of avoiding excessive administrative work it is not uncommon to impose a service qualification so that short-stay employees are never admitted and when there is a service qualification it is sometimes, but not always, the practice to count the qualifying period for pension purposes.

Even though there may be age or service qualifications for pension purposes, it is becoming increasingly the practice to admit all employees for life assurance benefit immediately they join the company.

TEMPORARY ABSENCE

If an employee is temporarily absent either for sickness or any other reason, he may remain a member even though no remuneration is paid so long as there is a definite expectation of return to service. No limit need be set if absence is caused by ill health so long as there is an expectation of return to work, but absence for any other reason should not normally exceed 3 years.

TYPES OF SCHEME

Occupational schemes fall into two main groups:

(a) statutory schemes set up for employees of public authorities or nationalised industries;

(b) private schemes set up either by individual employers for their own employees or by groups of employers for employees of the group or what are called federated schemes for employees of employers in a given trade.

These private schemes may be operated in any of three ways:

(a) the benefits may be insured through an insurance company under any one of a number of different types of contract;

(b) they may be privately administered by the employer who, subject to actuarial and investment advice, will make his own arrangements for providing the benefits and will run all the risks attendant thereon but should have the possibility of saving in cost;

(c) they may be of a hybrid between (a) and (b) known as a Managed Fund, whereby the scheme is operated through the medium of an insurance company, merchant bank, or some such institution which will provide expert advice on investment, actuarial, and the administration of the scheme. Basically, a managed fund is a self-administered scheme with an insurance company acting as an investment manager, and it is worth noting that actuarial and other professional advice may be provided independently of the insurance company.

However operated, the new code scheme will have two essential pieces of documentation if it is to secure all the relevant tax reliefs:

(a) it must be constituted under an irrevocable trust usually in the form either of a trust deed or a declaration of trust;

(b) it must have a set of rules.

The details of the scheme must be formally made known to the members. In the case of a new scheme this is usually done in the form of an announcement which is in due course followed up by a booklet setting out the provisions of the scheme in simple terms. Sometimes the booklet itself is the announcement.

Suffice it to say here that all documents must be drawn in such a manner as to meet the requirements of the Superannuation Funds Office and the Occupational Pensions Board, although, of course, the trustees of the scheme have certain discretionary powers.

COMMENT

One cannot disguise the fact that it is a highly complex matter to design a pension scheme so that it will meet the requirements of the Superannuation Funds Office, the Occupational Pensions Board, and also, as far as possible, the differing needs of the working populace.

The unions' objectives are straightforward enough: the equal opportunity for all to obtain a worthwhile level of retirement benefits —men and women, staff and hourly paid—in private and public sections of employment.

Equally, it is understood that there is the need to observe the limitations and requirements of legislation for the purpose of obtaining and retaining the taxation advantages of a scheme being "exempt approved".

A SUMMARY OF CURRENT LEGISLATION AS IT CONCERNS PENSIONS SCHEMES

This summary is a guide to current legislation and draws attention to the *maximum* benefits that can be included in a pension scheme to receive "exempt approval" from the Inland Revenue Authorities. *It should not be used in support of a pension claim upon an employer.*

FINANCE ACTS 1970 AND 1971 (KNOWN AS "NEW CODE" APPROVAL)

The Inland Revenue is empowered to grant:

EITHER *Approved* status to a pension scheme under which the employers' contributions are not regarded as additional income to employees for the purpose of determining their income tax liability;

OR *Exempt approved* status which has the additional advantages of the pension fund's assets not being liable to capital gains tax and the investment income being free from income tax deduction; furthermore, members are granted tax relief on their contributions.

The main requirements for "exempt approved" are:

Irrevocable trust—The pension scheme must be established under an irrevocable trust.

Employers' contributions—The employer must make contributions to the scheme.

Death-in-service-benefits—The lump-sum benefit must not exceed four times the deceased member's final remuneration, in addition to which a refund of the member's contribution with interest may be made. In addition, widows'/widowers' pensions not exceeding two-thirds of a member's anticipated pension may be paid.

Benefits at normal retirement—A tax-free lump-sum benefit must not exceed one and a half times final remuneration. The maximum retirement pension, including the pension equivalent of any lump-sum benefit, must not exceed two-thirds of final remuneration. In addition, widows'/widowers' pension not exceeding two-thirds of a member's pension may be paid.

Early retirement—Except on the grounds of medically certified incapacity, an early retirement pension is not allowed before age 50.

Leaving service (see also preservation requirements below)—Any cash refund on leaving service must be limited to the member's own contributions with interest if provided by the rules of the scheme. A refund of contributions is not permitted if a member's pensionable pay has ever exceeded £5000 in a twelve-month period—a preserved ("frozen") pension or a transfer payment to another exempt-approved fund has to be arranged.

PRESERVATION—SOCIAL SECURITY ACT 1973 (EFFECTIVE DATE 6 APRIL 1975)

The Act requires pension schemes to offer preserved ("frozen") pensions to scheme members leaving service over the age of 26 with a minimum of 5 years of pensionable service. Preserved pensions have to commence at the scheme's normal retirement age, and are normally to be calculated in the same manner as for normal retirement although based on completed pensionable service. It is necessary, however, to provide for early leavers with an entitlement to "short-service benefit" the same options for early retirement as are available to scheme members generally.

The Act does not permit scheme members leaving service after 5 April 1980 with at least 5 years of pensionable service to have a refund of contributions paid after 6 April 1975.

All other Inland Revenue and Occupational Pensions Board requirements are detailed at length in IR 12 (October 1974) known as the Practice Notes—obtainable from the Joint Office of Inland Revenue Superannuation Funds Office and Occupational Pensions Board, Apex Tower, High Street, New Malden, Surrey KT3 4DN.

CHAPTER 4

The Communication Exercise

THE NEED AND THE VALUE

Anyone with but the slightest interest in the subject is aware that pensions are a complex subject—but it need not be communicated to members and potential beneficiaries in a manner guaranteed to confuse. Repeated mention is made of the 65,000 schemes covering 11 million members, and such limited random sampling that has been done indicates that a substantial majority of members do not understand their entitlements and benefits, the reason for this being ineffective communication rather than mass disinterest.

To set about improving knowledge and, where necessary, interest, there is a need to provide—to use the emotive phrase—"a full disclosure of information". Not, in this instance, in the negotiating sense but on the simple premise that each member should have in his or her possession an explanatory booklet providing in clear, non-technical jargon full details of the scheme. The member should upon request also be supplied with a copy of the deed and rules. Annually a statement of benefits should be issued to each member covering the features upon which his or her interest is concentrated:

BENEFITS payable   on DEATH IN SERVICE
or at NORMAL RETIREMENT AGE
or upon LEAVING SERVICE PRIOR
TO RETIREMENT AGE

and the total of the member's contributions during the year.

Annual statements of account and periodic actuarial reports in a simplified presentation should also be distributed to members, not least for the purpose of establishing the cost to the employer, leaving no doubt, in the case of a good scheme, of the real value of the deferred-pay concept. One can be repeatedly surprised by the number of leading national companies who are prepared to invest millions in a good pension scheme but will not invest even hundreds in communicating the fact to their members. But the same companies seemingly go to endless cost in keeping their shareholders fully informed in glossy style.

Negotiated schemes that are inadequately communicated are neither appreciated nor understood by the members. A one-off distribution of an explanatory booklet, no matter how good, is not enough.

A consultative or advisory committee structure, going down to shop-floor level, is important in a company of any size in order to create awareness of the usefulness of and the problems associated with the members' scheme. The same procedure allows for a feed-back of problems, worries, or dissent from the shop floor.

I would expect the representatives on any joint pensions advisory committee to include in their discussions the problems of investment, the significance of wage and salary increases on the cost of final salary schemes against the background of an abnormal or spluttering rate of inflation, and the necessity of increasing pensions already in payment and the difficulties associated with doing this.

There is considerable experience now among large companies of member trustee participation and pensions advisory committee structures, some of which are commented upon in the chapter on member participation.

AIDS TO COMMUNICATION

This section deals mainly with communications on paper and illustrates by example the kind of documentation required to simplify and explain, and not to leave the average member in a state of confused perplexity.

To communicate well is to embrace information, education, and training in a form that will convince. Pensions should not be shrouded with mystique. Mumbo-jumbo or jargon merely creates suspicions. Why camouflage the basic fact that for each £1 invested by the member the employer is adding £2 (or whatever)?

Some of the documentation provided by pensions professionals to management and unions in connection with the consultation procedure under the Pensions Act is complicated in the extreme. Here was an excellent opportunity to simplify complicated formulae and to establish a simplified method of approach.

To illustrate:

The Social Security Pensions Act 1975 provides for a reduction of 7% in Social Insurance contributions (4½% employer, 2½% member) on earnings between the lower and upper limits if contracted out of the State scheme from or after April 1978. (The lower earnings limit is the approximate equivalent of the single person's flat-rate pension at the commencement of an income tax year; the upper earnings limit is approximately seven times the lower limit.)

This is the essential point to make in presenting the contract-in or contract-out choice, not a comparison between Social Insurance contributions with or without occupational scheme contributions (net of tax) before and after April 1978 (or whenever the decision is to be effective). The reduction (or abatement) figure of 7% is as fixed as one can reliably predict upon any politically exposed factor, at least it would seem for the first 5 years of operation of the Castle Plan, whilst Social Insurance contributions will increase regularly and tax relief on occupational scheme contributions will vary with budgets and personal circumstances.

The individual member, therefore, needs to know that if contracted out of the State scheme 2½% less is paid to the State on earnings between the lower and upper earnings limits BUT $X\%$ will be paid to the Company scheme (which is the equivalent of $x\%$ after allowing for full *current* tax relief) for benefits including the following which would NOT otherwise be provided by the State scheme (here list those applicable to the particular scheme), e.g. lump-sum benefit on death-in-service; widows'/dependants' pensions and children's allowances based on potential service, i.e. service that would have been fulfilled between the date of death and normal retirement age; early retirement pensions due to ill health, redundancy, or of own accord; the option to exchange part of the retirement pension for a tax-free cash sum subject to meeting the requirements for contracting out and Inland Revenue formula.

THE EXPLANATORY BOOKLET ISSUED TO MEMBERS

It is so easy to make the explanatory booklet as difficult to understand as a word-for-word copy of the trust deed and rules. That not being the purpose, what is the best way of preparing a booklet in an easy-to-read form that will not be mistaken for the deed and rules? This is a most important point because unless the booklet clearly states that the trust deed and rules are the only legal governing documents, in the hands of the "barrack room lawyer" it can be construed in a manner guaranteed to provide understandable discontent.

The purpose of the booklet is therefore to assist the member to understand more easily the main provisions of the scheme. It should answer basic questions, such as:

- How does the scheme work?
- Who is eligible to join?
- What do I have to pay?
- What are the benefits?
- How can I calculate my pension?
- Are my dependants protected whenever I die, either before or after retiring?
- What happens if I am away sick for a long period?
- What happens if I should leave the Company?
- Can I retire earlier than the stipulated age?

- Can I take a lump sum?
- How do I join?

The answers, whilst being in understandable language, should not "talk down" to employees, and whilst pictorial inserts can assist, they should not be of the "Mickey Mouse" variety. I have known shop-floor representatives to express considerable anger at communication exercises aimed at seemingly sub-normal levels of intelligence.

To illustrate: the answer to the question "How can I calculate my pension?" can be expressed in this way:

"Your pension is the answer to the following formula: 1/60th of final pensionable earnings times pensionable service. This is not quite as complicated as it might appear. Your *final pensionable earnings* are EITHER your pensionable earnings for your last year before normal retirement date OR the average of your best three consecutive years'pensionable earnings in the last 10 years before your normal retirement date, *whichever is the higher.* Your pensionable service is the total of continuous years between the date you join this scheme up to your normal retirement date."

The explanation may then continue to illustrate the arithmetic:

"Unless you are within a year or two of normal retirement date, estimating final pensionable earnings with any accuracy will be difficult. As a guide, however, a useful comparison with your latest pensionable earnings can be made by using the figure shown on your last income tax return. Let us assume your pensionable earnings for last year were £3000 and that your pensionable service at age 65 will total 30 years and insert these figures in the pensions formula. The result would be as follows:

1/60th of £3000 × 30 = your pension = £1500 per year."

A booklet written in this style can deal with otherwise complicated preservation requirements of the Social Security Act 1973 under a series of subsections, for example:

LEAVING THE SERVICE OF THE COMPANY

- Your rights preserved.
- When a cash refund of your contributions *is* possible.
- Death before retirement.
- The alternative to freezing your benefits—transferring the benefits to another employer's scheme.

ANNUAL STATEMENT OF BENEFITS

A specimen form (as illustrated overleaf) should be suitable for other than the most uncooperative computer. It is recognised that some pension funds provide an even more detailed annual statement, but the majority of funds have not made a practice of keeping individual members up-dated with advice on their entitlements in the manner suggested.

Many an "instant" widow, where the possibility of the death of the breadwinner had never been considered, let alone discussed, would have been saved considerable mental anguish in addition to the bereavement had she the prior knowledge of her financial position in widowhood. The "backwoods" viewpoint is that many husbands would never discuss these matters with their wives, but are we not seeking to extend communications to potential beneficiaries and dependants as part of the extension of education in pensions?

The worker who saves in the building society, the bank, or practically any other investment medium has easy access to records of his accumulated "nest egg". Similarly, the worker contributing part of his immediate pay, together with his deferred pay, to a pension scheme should receive regular statements at least of current entitlements.

FORM OF WISH (IN RESPECT OF DEATH-IN-SERVICE LUMP-SUM BENEFITS)

The specimen annual statement of benefits contains a reminder in

SPECIMEN FORM ILLUSTRATING THE INFORMATION A PENSION SCHEME
MEMBER SHOULD RECEIVE ANNUALLY

THE XYZ PENSION SCHEME STATEMENT OF BENEFITS		
Member's name Reference No./Clock No. National Insurance No.		
Year ended		
Pensionable earnings during year	£	
Total pensionable service to date	Years Months	
Total member's contributions during year	£	
Annual pension accrued to date payable from normal retirement date	£	
Death-in-service benefits: Lump sum Dependant's pension	£ £	 per annum
Estimated annual pension assuming no change in annual pensionable earnings and contributions continue to normal retirement date	£	

Notes:
1. This statement replaces any other previously issued and it is suggested it should be kept with your copy of the pension scheme booklet.
2. Any questions that you have to ask on this statement should be raised directly with. . . . .
3. Have you completed the form indicating to whom you would wish the death-in-service benefit to be paid? It may be amended should you wish to make an alteration.

Date of Issue   XYZ PENSION TRUSTEE CO. LTD.

(The statement should also show clearly the position *re* return of member's contribution (where appropriate) and the scheme's preservation provisions.)

respect of the possibility of changing previously expressed wishes in the event of death-in-service benefit becoming payable. It is surprising how this, normally regarded, essential part of keeping a member in touch with the pension scheme is frequently overlooked or ignored. Misunderstandings can easily be aroused when referring to trustees' discretionary powers, and a carefully worded announcement should accompany the form upon which the member is invited to express his wish. Explanation should be given that the discretionary powers are confined as to *whom* the lump sum should be paid to, not as to *how much* is to be paid in total.

The purpose of giving trustees these discretionary provisions in respect of lump-sum death benefits is to avoid (quite legally) the payment of capital transfer tax—formerly estate duty. Furthermore, the fact that the lump sum does not form part of the deceased's estate enables, in the vast majority of cases, payments to be made promptly and with a minimum of the delay normally associated with obtaining grant of probate or letters of administration.

It is useful to give guidance upon the range of beneficiaries that the trustees would bring into their considerations should it not be a clear-cut case (and the greatest proportion are) OF THE LUMP SUM BEING PAID TO A WIDOW OR WIDOWER. For example: the beneficiaries shall include the employee's widow or widower; any former wife or husband of the employee; the following relatives of the employee (whether by birth or adoption) born at any time, namely issue, parents, issue of parents, step-children, and issue of step-children; the spouses, widows, and widowers of the said relatives; any other individual whose name has been notified to the Trustee Company in writing by the employee prior to his or her death as being a person the employee wishes the Trustee Company to consider as a possible recipient of the sum; any other person who in the opinion of the Trustee Company was dependent wholly or partially on the employee for the ordinary necessities of life suitable for persons in his or her class and position, and so on.

(Note: The above wording is provided for illustrative purposes only. It is not suggested that the wording is legally exact. A member

of the legal profession should be consulted to draft documentation to be used in practice.)

The form of wish should of course include a statement to the effect that the member understands the request is not to be binding on the trustees, but in the event of death while a member of the scheme, the member would like the trustees to consider making payment of the lump-sum benefit to the person(s) named. It is helpful to include yet a further reminder that in the event of any change in circumstances it is the member's responsibility to see that any alteration in the wishes should be made known to the trustees by submitting a further form expressly cancelling the original.

ANNUAL STATEMENT OF ACCOUNTS

The average accounts and balance sheet are understood only by those equipped with the knowledge to extract the relevant information. Here there is scope to introduce pictorial diagrams to supplement a simplified form of accounts which should be included in addition to the audited accounts.

The accounts in easily understandable form can be rounded off to the nearest £1000 and be produced in this way, as the balance sheet example shows:

BALANCE SHEET FOR THE YEAR ENDED 31 DECEMBER 197– –

Income	£	Expenditure	£
The Company's contributions	1,230,000	Pension payments	195,000
Members' contributions	602,000	Death benefits	418,000
Income from investments	410,000	Refunds and transfers	52,000
Transfers from other schemes	45,000	Balance transferred to fund to provide your future benefits	1,622,000
Total received during year	£2,287,000		£2,287,000

These accounts, reproduced in a folder, can usefully include:

- The investment manager's report.
- Details on membership changes.
- Member trustees' report.
- Actuarial comment.
- Details of pensioners (who should also receive a copy).

KEEPING IN TOUCH WITH PENSIONERS

A neglected area in the communication chain is the pensioners—those without whose past endeavours there would, in all probability, be no pension scheme and no company. There are some excellent examples where employers or pension funds keep in close contact with pensioners. Regular visits are made, at least yearly, to ascertain if any assistance can be provided. The visitor needs to be fully acquainted with the pensioner's locality and be able to give advice on supplementary benefit entitlements and similar matters. With the expansion of member participation in pension consultative structures the pensioner's viewpoint should not be overlooked—if it is, then it is to be hoped that the pensioners themselves ensure that provision is made for suitable representation from time to time.

COMMENT

As a nation we throw up examples of the lack of communication—the inability of spanning generation gaps, families who do not converse, the millions who watch and never participate because of the influence of the "box".

Pensions had been treated in the same degree of neglect until legislation enabled the unions to bring the subject to the negotiating table. A small percentage of the entire workforce, unionised or not, will continue to rely on the State in their retirement years. Even some of the best occupational schemes on a voluntary membership basis have only attracted from 60% to 80% applications in the past.

Over recent times there has been strong evidence that a scheme that is negotiated with the unions, jointly communicated with the unions at the outset (see examples that follow of typical questions raised at pension meetings together with suggested answers) together with member representation in a meaningful manner in a consultative trustee structure is almost certain of a successful launching. Therefore it is dependent upon the continuing exercise of COMMUNICATION.

THE COMMUNICATION EXERCISE: QUESTIONS AND ANSWERS

The following are examples of actual questions raised at meetings by potential or existing members of schemes, the meetings being of either an explanatory and/or introductory nature or "rescue" missions. Rescue in the sense that as misgivings over the introduction of a pension scheme were endangering industrial relationships, national union officials were charged with answering questions that might otherwise have been directed at management.

Examples given have been selected deliberately, being of a general nature, excluding questions applicable to specific schemes. They emphasise the need to communicate clearly and concisely, yet underline the high level of interest shown in pensions on the "shop floor".

ADDITIONAL VOLUNTARY CONTRIBUTIONS

Question: What are the disadvantages of making additional voluntary contributions?

Answer: The provision for additional voluntary contributions quite often leads to misunderstanding and unrest on the part of the members. Additional voluntary contributions to a pension scheme are subject to precisely the same income tax legislation as ordinary contributions, hence they cannot be refunded whilst the member remains in service. Similarly, additional voluntary contributions have to be subject to the same preservation (frozen pension) requirements as ordinary contributions to the scheme. A low proportion of members of pension schemes have been found to take advantage of additional voluntary contributions although full tax relief is granted subject to normal plus additional contributions not exceeding 15% of pay.

DEATH IN DEFERRED RETIREMENT PERIOD

Question: If I remain in service after the normal retirement age I understand my pension is increased. Will the 50% widow's pension also be increased?

Answer: Yes—the 50% widow's pension should normally be based on the pension earned at the actual date of retirement. You are correct in stating that your pension will increase for up to 5 years of service beyond normal retirement age. It should, however, be borne in mind that a person may receive an occupational scheme pension from normal retirement age and continue in some form of employment. The occupational pension is always subject to income tax deduction as earned income, i.e. the pension is added to the State pension plus any other earned income and tax deducted in PAYE fashion after allowing for personal and other tax reliefs.

DEATH IN SERVICE

Question: How is the lump-sum benefit disposed of should there be no obvious next of kin, or the next of kin dies simultaneously, say in a traffic accident?

Answer: The payment of the lump-sum benefit will be the subject of exhaustive and individual inquiries made by the trustees (and pensions advisory committees where appropriate) to establish *bona fide* dependants as beneficiaries. The death-in-service rule of a pension scheme describes in detail all of those to be regarded as potential beneficiaries.

EXEMPT APPROVAL

Question: Why is it necessary for a pension scheme to be subject to the requirements of the Inland Revenue?

Answer: A pensions fund has to be subject to the requirements of the Inland Revenue Authorities (and the Occupational Pensions Board) in order to obtain and maintain approval for tax purposes, which are:

    (1)   members' contributions ranking for full tax relief;
    (2)   employer's contributions not being assessable as income of the employees;
    (3)   interest income received and capital gains made by the pension fund are free from tax;
    (4)   pensions are treated as earned income subject to PAYE;
    (5)   the employer's contributions are allowed as an expense of trade.

FINAL PENSIONABLE SALARY FORMULA

Question: Why adopt the best three consecutive years in the last 10 (13) years of service as a final pensionable salary definition?
    Does the formula not operate unfairly in the case of:

    (a)   those who have long periods of absence due to ill health during the last 10 (13) years;
    (b)   those who have to accept lower paid employment for one reason or another during the last 10 (13) years;
    (c)   the consistent plodder whose pension expectations will be less than a colleague whose earning capacity increases

substantially for a period of three or more consecutive years during the last 10 (13) years of service;

(d) the man of 55 years of age or more who will in all probability reduce his life expectation by doing more overtime during his remaining years of service than he did when he was 25–35 years old simply to achieve a good average final salary?

Answer: This "final" pensionable earnings formula is the one that has been almost universally adopted for hourly paid workers throughout the United Kingdom—particularly in the engineering industry. It is a formula approved by the Inland Revenue Authorities, and is the stated objective of the TUC and constituent unions. It is because of the known fluctuation in overtime earnings and possible declining health of manual workers in later years that the formula is regarded on balance as being a fair one. (*Note:* In certain industries it may well be that a revalued average earnings scheme (on a basis similar to the additional component in the State scheme) will be the better method upon which to base pensions for hourly paid workers. A close examination of wages, earnings, and age structures in each case is necessary to determine the formula most appropriate to the particular circumstance.)

INTEGRATION WITH THE STATE SCHEME

Question: Why is the scheme integrated with the State basic pension? Surely the effect of the State basic offset from pensionable pay will be to reduce a member's pension expectations from the Company?

Answer: The two-tier State system of pensions (from April 1978) is an integrated one. When introducing an occupational scheme for the first time to employees who have not been accustomed to paying contributions, can it be anticipated that all would be prepared to pay contributions to both the State and the occupational scheme on that part of earnings related to the basic flat-rate State benefit? (*Note:* Integration is perhaps the most difficult aspect of pensions to negotiate in a manner acceptable to any group of workers. Thereafter the communication problem is no less difficult.)

INCOME TAX RELIEF ON MEMBERS' CONTRIBUTIONS

Question: Please explain the extent of the tax relief allowed on members' contributions and say why this item is not recorded on employees' pay packets.

Answer: Members' contributions are allowed in full against PAYE earnings. It is standard practice for an employee's gross earnings to bear the deduction of the pension contribution *before* the employer deducts income tax in accordance with each individual's PAYE code number. You should be able to check that your tax calculation has been suitably amended at the Pay Office.

INSURED SCHEMES

Question: Which insurance company is involved in the pension plan and does the Company hold any type of share in the insurance company concerned? Alternatively, does the insurance company concerned have a major shareholding in our Company? If the insurance company concerned does have investment in the Company does the pension fund benefit from the profit of that investment and will the extent to which the fund gains be shown in the annual report?

Answer: It is not appropriate to give a standard answer to this question. Nevertheless, that this kind of question is frequently asked can but be indicative of strained industrial relations, charged as it is with suspicion.

INVESTMENTS

Question: How are the monies invested? What is the total percentage of the fund invested in any one stock, unit trust, etc?

Question: Are details of the portfolio to be disclosed to each fund member?

Question: Are there any reserves to provide against poor investment returns and, if at any time the trust fund is insufficient to meet its commitments, will it mean further increases in members' contributions?

Question: Does the fund invest in or lend money to the Company? If so, why?

Question: Can the trust fund lend money to a trade union?

Question: Does the fund have to carry the trust company's administration costs? If so, what percentage of the whole is this likely to be and how will it compare with the administrative costs of a unit trust?

Answers: These matters are ones that the trustees (investment and local pensions advisory committees) should take in the ordinary course of business. Part of the function of membership participation must be to give all members greater access to and understanding of the fund's financial position. It has to be borne in mind that trustees have to conduct their affairs in a prudent and impartial manner. With the aid of appropriate advice, investments have to be secure and arranged as far as possible to meet the capital growth and income requirements that the consulting actuary calculates as being necessary to keep the fund viable.

PENSIONABLE EARNINGS

Question: Why relate pensionable earnings and final pensionable earnings to gross PAYE and not to the standard basic pay for a normal week?

Answer: It is the objective of the TUC and all constituent unions for pensions to be related to gross earnings.

Question: Similarly, why not impose a "ceiling" limit on the amount of contributions any members should be required to pay?

Answer: In addition to the answer to the previous question the introduction of an "offset" to take account of the State pension results in members' contributions being partially controlled in amount.

PRESERVATION AND THE SOCIAL SECURITY ACT 1973

Question: What is meant by preservation?

Answer: The Social Security Act 1973 preservation requirements applicable from April 1975 require as a minimum that members withdrawing from pensionable employment must be provided with a "frozen" (preserved) pension if they have given 5 years of pensionable service and they are aged 26 or over when leaving. The constituent unions of the TUC argue that all employers' contributions are deferred pay to which the pension scheme member should be entitled at all times; hence, it should be an increasing practice to negotiate that *regardless* of age or length of service schemes will provide a frozen pension when a member leaves the Company before retirement.

PRESERVED PENSIONS

Question: What happens to the pension in the case of employees who leave service before pension age and have accrued preserved pension rights but thereafter cannot be traced?

Answer: The trustees and the Company will have to use their best endeavours to trace their former employees who, in turn, should register changes of address with the Company in order to facilitate the eventual payment of pensions.

RETURN OF CONTRIBUTIONS—THE "£5000 RULE"

Question: Why is there a rule preventing a refund of members' contributions under any circumstances for those earning over £5000 per annum?

Answer: This is a restriction imposed by the Inland Revenue Authorities to all approved schemes; it is not peculiar to any one scheme. Whilst the restriction appears to limit freedom of choice by compelling the taking of a preserved pension, it does prevent abuse of tax-relief advantages.

NON-RETURN OF MEMBERS' CONTRIBUTIONS
WHEN EMPLOYMENT CONTINUES

Question: Why cannot we have our money back from the previous scheme now that we are contributing to a new one?

Answer: The trustees would act in breach of trust if they attempted to refund contributions to members on the commencement of a new scheme. It is illegal to refund contributions to a member who is remaining in employment.

PROOF OF AGE

Question: Why must my date of birth be proved before I can receive a pension from the scheme?

Answer: Because your entitlements and benefits are related directly to your age.

RETIREMENT OVERSEAS

Question: What happens to the pension entitlement of (a) an immigrant returning to his native land? (b) a British citizen emigrating?

Answer: Although the pension is payable from the United Kingdom, provided the returning immigrant or the departing emigrant gives full details to the trustees, the pension will be paid to an overseas bank subject to prevailing Bank of England Exchange Control conditions. This procedure applies equally to a preserved pension, payable at normal retirement age, or to an immediate pension.

COMMENT

This selection of Questions and Answers, whilst typical, cannot hope to cover all the points likely to be raised. Time could be well spent in preparing in advance of meetings the responses to queries ranging over:

(1) Deductions from holiday pay scheme entitlements.
(2) Early retirement due to redundancy, ill health, or of own accord.
(3) The position of common law wives.
(4) Escalation of pensions in payment.
(5) Past service of older employees.
(6) Temporary absence.
(7) Past discriminations against manual workers and/or female employees.

Plus, of course, the answers to the fundamental questions:

What do I or my dependants get, if:

I live to retirement age;
I die before reaching retirement age;
I quit the service of the Company;

and HOW MUCH WILL IT COST ME and THE COMPANY?

CHAPTER 5

Membership Participation

In June 1976 the Department of Health and Social Security published a White Paper entitled *Occupational Pension Schemes: the role of members in the running of schemes*. In fact it covered a considerably wider area than that, dealing also with issues of disclosure of information and solvency. In brief it covered the following areas:

DISCLOSURE OF INFORMATION

The Government proposed legislation to ensure that members of occupational schemes were provided with full information about the running of schemes, their benefits, the methods of financing, and investment. They took the view that members ought as a matter of justice, and in the interest of good relations between employers and employees, to be given all the information necessary to enable them to feel an involvement in how schemes operate and they will be affected personally.

Members of schemes already have a legal right to certain information, but the White Paper said: "We need to go further still. All employees in schemes should get the kind of information which only the most fortunate now receive. There must be systematic arrangements for disclosing the vital particulars about the administration and progress of an occupational pension scheme not only to all its members but in addition to recognised independent trade unions, who need it to protect the interests of their members.''

There were several types of information to which scheme members and their trade union representatives ought to have access:

(1) general information about the scheme, its benefits, method of financing, constitutional and management structure;
(2) the ongoing financial and actuarial situation of the scheme and the investment of its assets;
(3) information personal to the member, e.g. his own benefit position, should only be disclosed to the member.

The White Paper stressed: ''The Government considers that compulsory disclosure of information on the scale proposed is essential if workers and unions in all schemes are to be able, as only some of them are now, to play a responsible part in the running of pension schemes which so closely affect their interest. Workers will then be able to satisfy themselves that so far as possible adequate arrangements have been made to safeguard their pension rights.''

MEMBERSHIP PARTICIPATION PROPOSALS

The Government proposed that members of occupational schemes through their trade unions should have 50% of the membership of any controlling bodies specified by the legislation because, said the White Paper, ''there are many advantages in schemes being run jointly by employees and employers''. Legislation would be brought forward after discussions with interested bodies.

This partnership would give members of pensions schemes more confidence in them and a greater sense of security. It could also be expected to give them a better appreciation of the extent of the claims on resources constituted by pension schemes.

The White Paper stated:

''It is likely that the Employment Protection Act will increasingly secure that occupational pension schemes are brought into the sphere of collective bargaining. The normal position will then be that schemes, and alterations in schemes, will be negotiated by recognised independent trade unions. In that situation the Government believes that the best way of securing independence of those who are appointed, as a result of legislation, to achieve effective member representation in the running of schemes is to ensure that this is done through trade union machinery instead of leaving the employer to nominate them to decide on the arrangements.

"This would have the additional advantage of providing a means by which relatively large numbers of union members and officials, taking the country as a whole, would become familiar with the day to day problems of running particular pension schemes. While collective bargaining would no doubt usually be carried on by other union members or officials, the indirect results of having this body of up-to-date experience available for consultation could not fail to be beneficial.

"For these reasons, the Government is proposing that participation by employees in the running of occupational pension schemes should be achieved through the agency of recognised independent trade unions, and that they should have a right of appointment to 50 per cent of the membership of any controlling body or bodies specified by the legislation."

SOLVENCY

The Occupational Pensions Board, which had already examined the question of solvency, particularly in pension schemes which will be contracted out of the Government's new scheme, was now to be asked to study the question for schemes which will not be contracted out and report on any further legislative or other measures "directed to providing greater security for the pension rights and expectations of members". The findings of the OPB show that there is a long history of financial stability in the affairs of occupational pension schemes, that failures to pay benefits have been very few, and that this continues to be the case in spite of recent difficulties.

The White Paper went on to say: "It cannot be assumed, however, that because schemes have generally been able to meet their obligations in the past no action is necessary to ensure that they will continue to do so."

WOMEN

The Government's commitment to the principle that women should have a fair deal in occupational pension schemes was reiterated in the White Paper. In February 1975 the OPB were asked to consider and report on equality of status for men and women in occupational schemes. The OPB's report on this was almost completed, and the White Paper proposed that the same consultation process should cover this issue.

OCCUPATIONAL PENSIONS BOARD

The OPB has powers both to supervise and to assist occupational pension schemes, and in view of this the White Paper said it is important that both the constitution and membership of the Board should reflect the fact that employers have set up the schemes, invariably contribute to them, and often have major commitments under such schemes. The Government therefore intend to consult on any changes which may be desirable in the constitution of the OPB in the light of the new responsibilities the legislation will place on the Board.

TIME-TABLE

The proposed changes would give members of occupational pension schemes the right to know the essential facts about their schemes and to take part in running them. They must be introduced as soon as possible, but the time-table must be realistic, states the White Paper.

"In the next two years up to April 1978 those concerned with occupational pension schemes will be busy adjusting to the new State pension schemes, either through contracting out or through changes which may be necessary if they decide not to contract out. The Government consider that this must be a priority task in which scheme members, through their trade unions, should be actively involved. But while the Government would hope that the implementation of the new requirements would start straight away, these would not become compulsory in any event before April 1978 and the Government would undertake to give at least two years' notice before they did become compulsory. This would enable schemes either to make all the changes together, or to phase them in over a period.

"The first step will be for the Government to discuss the proposals in this White Paper with representative organisations, including the TUC, the CBI, and those concerned with occupational pension schemes. After taking account of views and comments, the Government will present the new legislation as early as possible."

Much of the White Paper was based on the February 1975 report of the OPB, entitled *Solvency, Disclosure of Information and Member Participation in Occupational Pension Schemes,* but in one crucial area the Government went beyond the Board's recommendations. This was, of course, member participation.

The Board's report stated:

"We are not at this stage recommending a statutory requirement for member participation, and we have explained why we have concluded that such legislation would be premature. But we have come down in favour of legislation about disclosure of information. Although many members in the larger schemes may already be covered by adequate disclosure and participation arrangements, the total package recommended would considerably advance the extent to which scheme members and their representatives in most schemes were involved in and understood the running of their schemes. In particular, we are recommending:

(a) A comprehensive list of information which should be available to members and, through them, to their representatives, either automatically or on request.

(b) An approach to the Advisory, Conciliation, and Arbitration Service (on the basis that pensions are an appropriate matter for collective bargaining) to ask that their guidelines should include some fairly detailed reference to the pensions information which should be made available for this purpose.

(c) Disclosure of the methods of appointment used at present for the management bodies of schemes—and therefore the extent of member participation.

(d) A code of good practice on member participation which, together with disclosure of information, should facilitate local collective bargaining aimed at securing the most appropriate method of participation.

(e) An extension of the existing training facilities for member and employer representatives.

(f) A continuing study over, say 5 years, to see whether statutory requirements on participation should be introduced at a later stage.''

The major differences, then, are that the Government is now proposing a *statutory* requirement for representation ''through the agency of independent trade unions''.

OPPOSITION TO THE WHITE PAPER'S PROPOSALS

The White Paper came under immediate and sustained attack. The National Association of Pension Funds, for instance, stated that (*Financial Times,* 28 June 1976) that: ''from initial responses to the

White Paper many funds are angry at the prospect of trade union officials, who are members of a particular pension scheme, possibly having a major say in the investment of funds, while non-union members of the scheme would have no representation.''

It suggested that the proposals were ''clearly counter counter-inflationary'' and would deter many employers without occupational pension schemes from introducing them.

The CBI decided to launch a major campaign on the issue, claiming (*Daily Telegraph,* 29 September 1976) that ''moves to give trade unions control of pension funds are as dangerous to Britain as schemes to nationalise banks and insurance companies ... while public attention was directed to the banking issue the pension fund proposals might slip through quietly and give unions power to dominate the financial scene with access to £20,000 million of other people's money.''

The Conservative Party also joined in the confrontation, with Mr. Patrick Jenkin, spokesman on social services, claiming (*The Times,* 1 October 1976): ''The sheer intolerance of this proposal is breathtaking. There are millions of pension schemes members who are not and have no wish to belong to a union. Are they to be disenfranchised?''

Much of the hostile comment indicated that the critics had either not read the document or that they know little or nothing about industrial relations. It is not proposed that full-time union officials should become trustees of 65,000 pension schemes. It would be an impossible task, practically speaking, even if that was what their members wished. In fact numerous discussions with existing member trustees have made it clear that they would themselves oppose any move to take the control of schemes from their hands into the hands of full-time officials; it would be a rash official who would endeavour to do so. Responsibility, rather than power, in the trade union movement fundamentally comes from below, and while it may seem to outsiders as if the leadership is unfettered by consideration of their members' reactions, in fact the leadership must be responsive if they are to retain their positions.

It is, of course, the Government's proposal that membership representation should be achieved ''through the agency of recognised independent trade unions"; in most cases it can be envisaged that it will be through the normal collective bargaining or consultative machinery used to discuss many other matters subject to joint regulations in enlightened companies today, and increasingly also in other companies through the workings of the Employment Protection Act. Later in this chapter detailed examples of cases where such joint regulation on pensions already exists are given.

A "RECOGNISED INDEPENDENT TRADE UNION"

At this juncture it may be helpful to look at what is meant by "recognised independent trade union". The phrase arises from the Employment Protection Act which for the first time gave a legal right to every independent trade union to take steps to obtain recognition. There is a lengthy and rather unsatisfactory procedure, culminating in a claim in the County Court which the General and Municipal Workers Union and other unions recommend should only be used when the usual industrial methods have failed. The diagram opposite summarises the procedure.

Independent is defined as meaning free from the control or influence of any employer. Case law on the subject is at an early stage, and there has been considerable controversy. The concept of conferring a certain legal status on trade unions and employee associations declared to be independent originated with the 1971 Industrial Relations Act. "Independent trade unions" were defined in the Act as "those not under the domination or control of an employer" and were granted a range of privileges and immunities—ignored in practice by TUC unions who did not register.

The Trade Union and Labour Relations Act 1974 re-defined "independent" by adding on to the Industrial Relations Act definition. The Trade Union and Labour Relations Act definition, which is the definition employed by the Certification Officer under the Employment Protection Act, is as follows: an independent trade union is one which "is not under the domination or control of an

RECOGNITION PROCEDURE

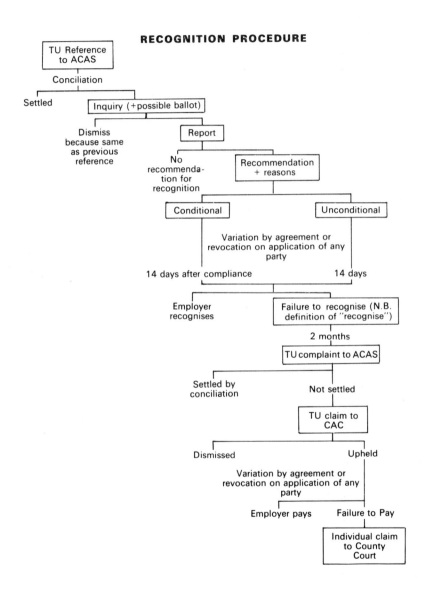

employer or a group of employers or one or more employers' associations; and is not liable to interference by an employer or any such group or association (arising out of the provision of financial or material support or by any other means whatsoever), tending towards such control''.

The Government's initial attempt to introduce supplemental criteria to the Trade Union and Labour Relations Act definition into the Employment Protection Bill which the Certification Officer would have had to take into account in deciding whether or not to give certificates to unions making applications, was unsuccessful. These criteria were largely drawn from a study on recognition published by the old Commission on Industrial Relations. The Certification Officer was therefore largely left to his own resources to devise criteria to apply in deciding whether or not unions satisfied the definition of independence contained in the Trade Union and Labour Relations Act. In doing so, however, he has not ignored the Commission on Industrial Relations' experience and, indeed, the criteria he is now applying do not appear to depart in any significant respect from the Commission on Industrial Relations' criteria. According to the Certification Officer his criteria are as follows.

ORGANISATION AND STRUCTURE

- Is membership open to employers, self-employed or senior members of management, and if so, what restrictions are there on the role of such members in the conduct of the union's affairs?
- Is there any evidence of the involvement of an employer or senior members of management in the establishment of the union or in the conduct of its internal affairs?
- Does the structure of the union or the number and role of its officials suggest undue reliance on an employer?
- How do the rules provide for the policy of the union to be determined?

- Do the rules contain provisions about any form of industrial action and, if so, what conclusions can be drawn from them?
- If procedure agreements, etc., have been submitted, what light do these throw on the union's status as an independent body, its involvement in genuine collective bargaining, and the facilities afforded to it by an employer?

FINANCE

- What are the main sources of the union's income?
- Do members' subscriptions represent a realistic level of income?
- Do the accounts indicate that the union may be receiving any form of financial support from an employer?
- Is the union's expenditure within its income and what are the capital reserves?
- Does the union have full-time officials, and what are the arrangements for the payment of officials whether full time or part time?
- What would be the effect on the union's finances of the withdrawal of whatever material or financial support is provided by an employer?
- Does the union have its own premises and, if so, how are they paid for?

A number of general points made by the Certification Officer relating to the application of these criteria in particular cases are worth noting, especially since some of these points relate to the objections raised by TUC unions. On the question of single company-based unions, he has stated: "We do not take the view that all 'single company' unions must of their nature be dependent on the employer; if we did it would rule out for example the Post Office Unions, and even the N.U.M. and the N.U.R. Clearly other factors must be taken into account as well. But on the face of it there may be a greater risk of employer interference in the case of single company unions—

especially if the union is small and has only modest resources—than in that of more broadly based organisations."

On the question of financial support from employer sources, he takes the view that if the cost of that support exceeds the union's own resources then there "must be a *prima facie* risk of employer interference". No single criterion is taken in isolation; it is a question of taking a balanced view on the weight of all the evidence. To the extent that some degree of subjective judgement is inevitable, it is important to ensure that such judgements are only made after full and careful investigation.

Whilst it is important to consider the origin of any union or association (i.e. the extent to which it was initiated by the employer) many associations evolve over a period of time from perhaps a consultative body to a negotiating body. It is therefore important to judge the state of development of such an association at the time of its making application for independence.

TUC unions have been pressing for an amendment to the Employment Protection Act's provisions on certification, and the Secretary of State for Industry recently announced that "the Government agree that the general legislation relating to certification of independence is unsatisfactory and needs tightening up. The existing provisions result in certificates being granted in circumstances where there is a risk of their being used to upset stable collective bargaining arrangements and to create damaging inter-union disputes." Clearly this statement implies that the Government is committed to introducing amending legislation of some sort in the relatively near future.

It is not clear what such legislation might say. Any criteria framed around general principles such as the need to maintain stable collective bargaining will run up against the problem that many non-TUC affiliates are already recognised and negotiating with employers.

The current definition should be the working basis. Is it that the Board, and many commentators, are confusing the meanings of negotiating and collective bargaining?

In classic industrial relations theory, as propounded by the Webbs, it was held that there was a "vital distinction ... between the making of a new bargain and the interpreting of a term of an existing one" (S.

and B. Webb, *Industrial Democracy*, 1902). But more recently "it has frequently and in my judgement, rightly, been said that the administration just as much as the making of rules is a part of collective bargaining, if only because in practice these two processes cannot be effectively separated" (Flanders, *British Journal of Industrial Relations*, Vol. 6, No. 1, March 1968).

Fundamentally we are talking about a primarily political institution, a method of making the rules involving a power relationship between institutions. (The often-used analogy of the market place is a mistaken one. Trade unions do not sell the labour of their members—they seek to influence the rules under which individual agreements involving labour are made.) What distinguishes collective bargaining from any other rule-making process in job regulation is, to quote Flanders again, "the *authorship* of its rules; the fact that they are jointly determined by representatives of employers and employees who consequently share responsibility for their contents and observance".

In recent years collective bargaining has extended its scope to include regulation of the role of management as well as regulations of labour markets. It is, it should be stressed, an extension rather than a qualitative charge. Nonetheless, in dealing with pension areas collective bargaining will change its *style* because of different demands being placed upon it. A "negotiating stance" is inappropriate on a board of trustees of a pension fund, but it is a part of the developing role of collective bargaining that the member trustee is there and is involved in administering the jointly agreed rules and trust deed.

THE AREAS OF MEMBERSHIP PARTICIPATION IN PENSIONS

What areas should member representatives on the Trustee Board concerned deal with? Here again it is useful to quote the Occupational Pensions Board report:

"Direct participation by member representatives on the management body concerned would be advantageous in the following areas:

(i)   operating the provisions of the scheme, by interpreting the rules to determine individual benefit rights, receiving special payments, voluntary contributions and transfer values for individual members, and awarding appropriate benefits, considering applications for early retirement on ill-health grounds, and permitting options under the scheme, for example, commutation or allocation, where these are not a right under the rules;

(ii)   operating discretionary powers involved in particular benefit payments, for example, deciding to pay a death benefit to a particular beneficiary or considering whether a member should be covered for a particular benefit on the basis of medical evidence;

(iii) disclosing scheme information to members whether on an *ad hoc* basis through the preparation of an annual report or other statements which would be required under our proposals or by some means; and

(iv)   broad investment policy within the powers laid down by the trust deed (the Board would expect that, in most cases, day to day investment decisions would, and should, be delegated to experts)."

A TRUSTEE'S RESPONSIBILITY

Essentially the responsibility of the trustee to the member is to administer the trust, that is the pension fund, to the best of his ability for the benefit of ALL the beneficiaries, that is ALL the fund members. He is not appointed to represent sectional interest. He cannot, he MUST NOT be better disposed, for example, towards members of trade unions as against non-union members, or the members of a particular trade union as against those of another union. I consider it essential that this should be stated carefully and clearly, and this is repeated on regular "Introduction to Pension Fund Trusteeship" courses held at the GMWU training college. It is no part of the trustees' duties or responsibilities to seek to negotiate improvements in the benefits or terms of the pension scheme. Their job, their sole job, is to administer the trust fund in accordance with its trust deeds and rules and general trust law. The unions will negotiate improvements in their members' schemes.

Any member who comes onto the Board of Trustees considering that he is playing the sort of negotiating role he may be used to in undertaking wage bargaining must disillusion himself very quickly. He is in a unique position of close co-operation with management as an equal—for management trustees of course must not favour the company's position especially either—and he is in the position of a reasonable and prudent man using his common sense to administer the fund and its benefits.

The fund or trust property must be administered in such a manner that the consequential benefits and advantages accrue not to the trustees but to the persons called beneficiaries—in the case of the pension fund, the members. A trustee may be a beneficiary, in which case advantages will accrue in his favour to the extent of his beneficial interest, that is to the extent, but ONLY to the extent, that he is entitled to benefit under the fund rules.

Trustees are dealing only with a very limited area. While the existence of member trustees may be valuable in itself, true membership participation can only arise when there is in addition a full pension negotiating and consultative structure. Without it either the trustee's role is strained to breaking point as he attempts to cope with differing demands, or he becomes isolated from the scheme's membership. Where we have a fully developed consultative structure, we have achieved this through the device of a two- or three-tier system pensions committee, at plant level, at divisional level if the size of the company justifies it, and at company-wide level. Members of the Board of Trustees, though they come up through the lower levels, are not usually allowed also to be members of the company-wide committee, specifically to avoid conflicts of interest. Sometimes it is this committee itself that negotiates improvements; sometimes they recommend to the Company's Joint Industrial Council. In general we rather tend to prefer the second as it puts pensions more clearly in the wage-bargaining arena.

Such a structure makes relatively easy the trustee's second main role—which is to know what the members really think. A criticism often made of worker directors in, for instance, the BSC experiment was that they became too remote and absorbed in technicalities, and did not understand what people on the shop floor really thought. A good trustee, whether springing from management or members, should make every effort to keep himself aware and informed of their views. He might be member of the plant-level committees, or he might be invited as an observer, or he might simply have informal meetings every so often. There are companies where the trustees hold a meeting and account for their stewardship to the whole membership —or as many as wish to go along—in each plant, and this practice is to be commended.

To receive genuine feedback it is important that the consultative committees have a real job of work to do and are not just "rubber stamps".

Even if there is no pensions consultative structure, regular pension discussions with shop stewards' committees can but improve understanding and thereby relationships. The area of discretionary benefits is one that it is particularly important for employee representatives to concern themselves with. In 99 cases out of a 100 there will be no problem. There will be a wife and children and no other possible claimants. The other 1% may well take up more time and trouble than all the rest. The man with no known dependants, the man with two families, one with a marriage certificate and one without, the member who has been supporting an elderly mother—all these are cases where the distribution of a sizeable lump sum will need care and can lead to dissension. Again, if member trustees and local advisory committees are involved, the solutions are far more likely to be accepted as fair by all the other members of the scheme who will have known the deceased far better than the administrator is likely to have known him.

It is likely, too, that the hourly paid member trustee will be in touch more with the problems raised by hourly paid workers than with those raised by managers—the issue of supplementary benefits and how they can be affected by a pension, the length of time an industrial injuries claim can take to be settled, the difficulties faced by a man who must retire early because of ill health. They can also be in touch with feeling about individuals: I have been told of one case, for instance, where a man died in a car accident, and within 24 hours his legal widow, whom he had not talked to for 20 years, had collected his week's wages, the week in hand and holiday money, and put in a claim for his lump-sum benefit, leaving standing the woman he had actually been living with. In that case, probably nothing could have been done given the speed at which it all happened. But with regard to the entitlements and rights under the pension scheme, the member trustee ought, if his lines of communication are properly open, to be able to deal properly with the situation.

Saying there is a particular role in the exercise of discretion, however, is not to say that is the *only* role. There are some cases where member trustees have concentrated on the welfare role to the exclusion of the administration of the fund to the extent that there has been no member trustee on the investment sub-committee. There are other cases where the employer has sought to establish that situation from the start. This is *not* generally acceptable. Member trustees should be fully involved in the question of investment. The fear is expressed by some employers and scheme administrators that this will lead to the placing of funds in unsound investments. There is no reason why it should and, indeed, my experience of member-controlled funds is of an entirely responsible attitude. There is, at any time, room for doubt as to what is genuinely a sound investment—as illustrated by the recent history of the collapse of some thought-to-be-sound financial institutions, and disagreement with one's professional advisers does not automatically mean irresponsibility. It is not the duty of trustees to be experts but to behave with reasonable prudence and common sense.

A SPECIAL ROLE FOR MEMBER TRUSTEES

Is there a special role for the member trustee? In a sense, of course, there is not—whatever a good *member* trustee should be doing a good *management* trustee ought to do too. But in another sense the member trustee, *as* a member, has a vital role. It can be stated very simply TO BRING THE PENSION FUND MEMBERS AND THE PENSION FUND TOGETHER. By personifying the pension fund, the member trustee can make it an understandable reality here and now. The member should no longer need to console himself with the thought that they "WILL MAKE IT ALL CLEAR TO HIM WHEN THE TIME COMES". As well as discharging his duties as defined, the member trustee can be a most valuable two-way channel of communication—fund to members/members to fund. He is, in fact, living proof that the fund is something more than promises on paper; that the fund is in good hands and is being properly administered; that the discretionary powers are being applied with tact, compassion, and a real understanding of how the other half lives.

Even the best pension schemes can go sour. There are a number of companies with good schemes for which the employers are paying substantial sums of money, but the schemes have accumulated layer upon layer of suspicion. The suspicion may not be the Company's fault, but whoever is at fault, the existence of 50% member trustees should provide a safeguard against it.

Member trustees have the power to make a *positive and constructive contribution towards the unification of management and workers— a contribution towards the plea of all persons of honest intent—a unified industrialisation.*

There is a modern tendency to justify all types of projects in terms of their "spin off" or advantageous side effects. The "spin off" sought *and* expected from effective joint participation in the management of GOOD occupational pension funds is twofold:

> *Firstly:* a greater appreciation of the value of the pension scheme and therefore a greater sense of long-term security.
>
> *Secondly: all other things being equal,* more stable industrial relations.

The late lamented Brian O'Malley, who was Minister of State for Social Security and who steered the Castle Act through Parliament, summed up the issues in this way in March 1975.

"The trade unions, and particularly those representing manual workers, are more active and more interested today in securing occupational pensions than ever before. They rightly see pension contributions and benefits as pay—deferred pay. Those contributions are therefore central to the collective bargaining process and should be treated as such. Sound pension provision of this kind can play an important role in the future of the nation. It means a better future in retirement and ill health for all people. It is conducive to good industrial relations. It adds to savings on which investment is based and it can operate as a potent weapon against inflation. Occupation pension provision has therefore a vital part to play in the development of a fair and firmly based prosperity in the future."

It is appropriate to look at examples of membership participation working in practice in the wider sense, i.e. the total consultative structure.

THE BRITISH LEYLAND PENSION CONSULTATIVE STRUCTURE FOR HOURLY PAID EMPLOYEES

Personal involvement in the negotiations and inauguration of this hourly paid pension scheme and the consultative structure provided first-hand knowledge of nearly 100,000 workers voluntarily joining a contributory scheme between June and September 1975 against a background of incessant industrial unrest. I accept that British Leyland, as one of the largest employers in the country, one with— now—a special financial and political relationship with the Government, and one with a particularly complex multi-union, multi-plant set up, is not typical. It is not claimed that the scheme is perfect, that it is the be all and end all of membership participation, or that it is a blueprint that must be followed word for word elsewhere. Obviously circumstances will differ between companies; the trade unions are not going to reject a good scheme for participation simply because it does not conform to some predefined rigid pattern. It is, however, worth studying the British Leyland consultation and trustee structure, firstly, to ascertain the lessons to be drawn from it, and, secondly, because the vast trade union membership in Leyland found this participation structure entirely acceptable.

The lowest tier of the British Leyland structure is the *Plant Pensions Advisory Committee* consisting partly of members elected by constituencies within the plants, partly by management. The Committee have the right to co-opt a pensioner if they wish. The exact composition of each committee at plant level is left flexible within broad guidelines to allow for variations in circumstances. The constitution provides for discussion on matters related to the administration of the pension scheme unless the item would unnecessarily involve the disclosure or discussion of confidential information regarding individuals' personal circumstances *without* their permission. Matters for regular consideration include: means of improving the administration and effectiveness of the pension scheme, pension matters upon which the Trustee Company or other appropriate bodies wish to have employees' views including matters related to discretionary benefits; the report of the Trustee Company and annual statements of accounts; developments in pension legislation and practice and related matters.

Items involving matters of wider interest than the individual plant may obviously be discussed at plant level but will be passed for consideration by a Group Pensions Advisory Council. The negotiated constitution stresses that it is not the function of a plant or group pensions advisory committee to negotiate on matters of improvement in or amendment to the rules of the scheme. Matters appearing in the minutes of these bodies are considered and discussed by a Joint Management Council consisting of management, full-time union officials, and elected members from the pension scheme. The consultative procedure booklet emphasises the fact that a representative must act on behalf of all members of the scheme irrespective of the trade union to which an employee belongs.

Above the Plant Committee is the *Group Pensions Advisory Committee*. There are three of these—one for each division. The arrangements for employee representation again are flexible to take in different circumstances in each division. Management is not allowed to appoint more members than their employee members to ensure that the 50/50 representation remains. The Group Committee has the right to co-opt specialist advisers as necessary.

FUNCTION OF THE GROUP PENSIONS ADVISORY COMMITTEE

(a) To discuss matters arising from the working of the pension scheme which have an implication/interest wider than a single plant.

(b) To co-ordinate and progress further recommendations upon improvements in the administration of the scheme or matters upon which the Trustee Company or other appropriate bodies wish to have employee views.

(c) To act as a channel of communication between the Plant Pension Committee and the Joint Management Council.

Items involving matters of wider interest than the individual group may be discussed, of course, but are passed for consideration to the Pension Schemes Joint Management Council. This is the top tier of this part of the structure.

THE JOINT MANAGEMENT COUNCIL

The Joint Management Council reviews all recommendations for improvement in the administration of the scheme and takes action accordingly, and reviews and approves as appropriate proposed changes in the rules of the scheme as recommended by the Corporation's Management, the trade unions, or the Trustee Company.

In doing so it will take into account the views of employees communicated through the committee structure. Consultations under the Social Security Pensions Act 1975 in reaching the contract-out recommendations were held within this negotiating body.

The constitution clearly establishes at all levels 50/50 membership participation throughout the pensions management structure. Over and above this, and separate from it, is the trustee structure. In this case there is a trustee company with a constitution providing for six directors from management and six from membership. The memorandum and articles of the company were also subject to negotiation and hence preserve a 50/50 situation at all times, for a quorum, the appointment of new trustees, and so on.

An explanatory consultative booklet sets out in clear non-legal language—and it is an example that others might do well to follow—the duties of the directors of the Trustee Company, including:

(1) To administer the scheme in accordance with the trust deed, the rules, the Finance Act 1970 and other relevant legislation, and to observe the requirements of the Superannuation Funds Office and the Occupational Pensions Board.

(2) To interpret the meaning of the rules where any questions of doubt arise.

(3) To modify, alter, or extend the rules subject only to the requirements that no amendment which increases British Leyland's financial liability may be made without its consent and to the requirement that recommendations for amendments will be mutually agreed between British Leyland and the trade unions through the medium of the Pension Scheme Joint Management Council.

(4) To keep and publish such accounts, registers, and records as are necessary for the proper administration of the scheme.

(5) To obtain an annual audit certificate of the fund's accounts.

(6) To invest the funds of the scheme.

(7)   To ensure that actuarial valuations are conducted.
(8)   To improve the benefits payable from any surplus funds that may be available to the scheme.
(9)   To exercise the discretionary powers defined in the trust deed and rules.

It would be incorrect to claim that this participation structure has worked completely smoothly: on the contrary, subsequent discussions have taken considerable time and patience and there have been a number of problems but none appear to be insoluble. The most time-consuming negotiations have surrounded the investment of the hourly paid pension scheme. During the original negotiations, spanning the period December 1973 to August 1975, the British Leyland management would agree only to the inauguration of an insured scheme despite the investment potential of the largest scheme ever negotiated in the United Kingdom. The unions reluctantly accepted this restrictive qualification to the agreement; refusal would, bluntly, have meant no scheme commencing in September 1975 and subsequently £2 million of death-in-service benefits would not have been paid in the first 12 months. Furthermore, 2 years of deferred pay by way of accrued pension entitlements would have been irretrievably lost for the 100,000 hourly paid members of the scheme. In the early part of 1977 negotiations for a switch to a "managed fund" basis were completed, being the "half-way house" until Leyland management has progressed to the position of equipping itself to operate the scheme on a self-administered basis— which clearly and expectedly has been the unions' objective since December 1973.

British Leyland's industrial relations problem, self-induced or otherwise, have not been increased by any inter-union rivalries on pension objectives and representation. The industrial relations situation is complex with numerous unions involved in more than 100 bargaining units. On pensions, however, there has been a general and workable acceptance by the unions for the single central bargaining body.

AN ILLUSTRATION OF PENSIONS ADMINISTRATION THROUGH EMPLOYEE PARTICIPATION

For the multi-plant company, much smaller than British Leyland, the following is a variation on the acceptance of the principle of employee participation: I contend that this type of structure can be designed to meet the particular requirements and circumstances— perhaps the first on these lines was negotiated by the unions with Massey–Ferguson, and many others are currently under negotiation. It will be noted that under this arrangement certain legal responsibilities and duties are delegated from the Trust Company to a Central Pensions Management Committee (eminently suitable where an external Corporate Trustee Company is used).

A Specimen Announcement of a Scheme for . . .

Pensions Administration through Employee Participation

In recognition of the trade unions' collective bargaining role in the area of pensions and in advance of legislation placing an obligation to provide members of the pension scheme with an opportunity to contribute to pensions administration, it is proposed to introduce a consultative structure within the Company, including the appointment of member trustees.

The proposal provides for the following structure:

Each location to have a Local Pensions Management Committee

Membership of this should be open to all members of the pension plan, but the nature of the representation and the number of members on the local committees should be determined in detail by local negotiation. In general, it should reflect trade union membership at location.

Where there are insufficient employees to justify the setting up of a local committee, a member representative should be elected from among the employees at that location.

The functions of a Local Pensions Management Committee will include:

(1)   a forum for the election of members' trustee representatives on the Central Pensions Management Committee;

(2)   provide such assistance to the Central Pensions Management Committee as the latter consider necessary for the successful conduct of their responsibilities and duties.

The chairman of the local committees shall be elected by those committees from among their members. The secretary should be a member of local management with responsibility for pensions matters, who shall be a non-voting member of the committee.

The Central Pensions Management Committee shall consist of:

The group pensions manager.

Two member and two management representatives from each location (appropriately qualified by total workforce).

One member and one management representative from each other location (to cater for representation from locations with a much smaller workforce).

The chairman shall be elected from the members and should have a casting vote where there is no consensus of agreement from the committee, which will meet at least quarterly.

The chairman, in conjunction with a non-voting secretary, who shall be appointed by the Company, is held responsible for agreeing the agenda in advance of the meeting.

The legal responsibilities and duties to be undertaken by the Central Pensions Management Committee on behalf of the Trustee Company, i.e. by delegated powers, shall be as follows:

(a)   the exercise of all discretionary powers of the Trustee Company relating to the disposal of benefits;

(b)   the interpretation of the rules in relation to any particular member, pensioner, or other beneficiary;

(c)   the entitlement to ill health early retirement pensions subject to a recommendation from the Company Doctor and the

Company's consent and, where necessary, having regard for other reliable medical evidence;

(d) to receive—for information—the audited accounts and actuarial reports;

(e) to make recommendations to the Company and the Trustee Company in connection with administration;

(f) to consider queries from members, pensioners, and other beneficiaries and to request any relevant information;

(g) to delegate to the Local Pensions Management Committee members at any of the establishments any of the aforesaid responsibilities and duties;

(h) to have no power to alter the provisions of the deed, rules, or collective agreement;

(i) the investment of the pension fund, to be undertaken in the first instance by the Investment Sub-committee with equal number of management and member trustees on it, plus specialist advisers as necessary.

Although members' representatives will be appointed from the separate establishments, once appointed they are in a trustee capacity as a result of which they must represent the interests of all beneficiaries.

(Note: The periods of office and subsequent appointments need to be negotiated with the unions to meet the circumstances of the individual company and its workforce.)

THE ROLE OF THE PENSIONS CONSULTATIVE STRUCTURE

Both examples given illustrate clearly the possibilities for company-wide structures in situations where the vast majority of bargaining is done at plant level. The question of company-level bargaining is one that worries many managements. They consider that it may upset delicately balanced established procedures, and may hold dangers of "leap-frogging" as the contact between different units of the same company grows. There can also be a real difficulty in defining terms of reference, where, for instance, in a large conglomerate, terms and conditions of different product divisions are settled in separate *national* negotiations. Without wishing to minimise these objections I would simply say that it is necessary for them to be overcome because there is no other way in which a single company-wide scheme can satisfactorily be dealt with.

Plant-level bargaining will produce unacceptable anomalies; at national level there will be no common ground between companies (as there is where you have a common minimum wage rate).

THE SELECTION OF MEMBER TRUSTEES

In the cases of Turner and Newall, GKN, and Leyland, and other industrial pension schemes, member trustees are appointed through an agreed selection procedure. In these cases, and others, a National Selection Committee was established, comprising equal numbers of union officials and management representatives. With the companies concerned the unions negotiated a basis of selection from nominations put forward by the scheme's members. I consider this procedure to be appropriate on the previously expressed understanding that trustees are not appointed to represent the members but to act as reasonable and prudent men in safeguarding the members' interests.

Provided that nominations are made by methods ensuring that applicants do have genuine local support, a selection procedure with detailed interviews is a proven way of choosing those who are not motivated for the wrong reasons. Answers to the following questions should enable a selection committee to assess if an applicant has the necessary blend of interest, knowledge, and judgement to cope with consideration of the complex issues that arise in a large pensions scheme.

TYPICAL QUESTIONS THAT SHOULD BE ASKED
OF TRUSTEE APPLICANTS

(1) Where does your interest in pensions stem from?
(2) Do you read articles, brochures, etc., on pensions? If so, which?

(3) What do you know about the State scheme starting in April 1978?
(4) Have you any views on contracting in or out of the State scheme?
(5) What is your understanding of the role of trustee?
(6) Have you any preconceived views on pension fund investments?
(7) In your opinion which is the most valuable benefit contained in the pension scheme of which you seek to be a trustee?
(8) The reverse—a benefit that should be introduced or improved?
(9) Do you think members would contribute more for an improved scheme?
(10) Will the duties of trustee, if you are appointed, interfere with any existing trade union involvement?

EDUCATION AND TRAINING

When the unions assess the right to equal representation on boards of trustees they are very conscious of the need for specialist training. The "rubber-stamp" type of trustee is not their objective, and a "rubber-stamp" trustee is certainly not undertaking his responsibilities seriously. The General and Municipal Workers Union has established regular training courses for trustees and intends to continue the practice. Other unions and the TUC also provide a number of courses.

The National Association of Pensions Funds in association with the Industrial Society run commendable courses and it is recognised that a considerable amount of in-service training is provided by enlightened employers. The Company Pension Information Centre, under the chairmanship of Lord Byers, is also doing a great deal in the field of education and training.

No matter to what extent other companies provide training for member trustees in the future, there will be a continuing role for the trade unions in education and training. This comes back to the need for the participation of members to be negotiated through the agency of trade unions rather than as individuals.

Meaningful democracy involves the control of resources. It involves the ability to get advice from an independent source and to have training and information that the members are prepared to trust. Much of the information available on pensions outside the trade union field is designed to sell—either the particular consultant's services or a prevailing orthodoxy about methods.

The unions may well—indeed they do—purvey the same sort of financial orthodoxy as management but they do not have the same axe to grind.

Non-trade unionists working within a consultative structure may well find themselves prey to unscrupulous insurance intermediaries. It is not unknown for an unsuspecting insurance company to be drawn into conflict with the unions at national level because a request to cross-quote at local level on inadequate information has sparked a potentially dangerous industrial relations situation. My advice to any insurance company is to provide a quotation only to full-time union officials who are in a negotiating situation with the Company concerned.

It is no secret that suspicion abounds at all levels within unions and amongst work people when pension schemes are inadequately communicated. I contend that one cannot separate communication from education and training, as a concerted effort on all of these facets would undoubtedly remove misplaced barriers and misgivings.

The General and Municipal Workers Union and other unions are seeking to provide this, but realise how little of the demand we can fulfil. Perhaps the BBC can be encouraged to put on follow-up programmes to its "Trade Union Studies" specifically upon pensions and related benefits, to be linked with a major education effort directed at the ordinary member?

A typical GMWU training syllabus for member trustees or members of pension committees, or indeed anyone with a pensions responsibility, includes the following:

(1)   Social Security Pensions Act 1975.
(2)   Pension scheme planning and design.

(3) Financial aspects of pension funds—why are they funded, actuarial methods, and valuations.

(4) Investment policy.

(5) Preservation—Social Security Act 1973.

(6) Legal responsibilities of fund trustees—discussion and role-playing participation.

(7) Exercise of discretionary powers—discussion and role-playing participation.

(8) Social security benefits in retirement.

Discussion on these courses, particularly during the role-playing sessions (which take the form of meetings of a "mock trustee board"), are lively and stimulating. Short courses such as these cannot turn out experts—they can merely kindle the flame of greater interest and awareness and advise sources for additional information. They must be only part of a much longer-term programme of training.

It is my firmly held view that given that training, members from the shop and office floor are equally able with management representatives to act as trustees in a responsible manner, prepared and able to take the necessary expert advice.

CHAPTER 6

Objectives and Realities in
Pension Negotiations

Realism in pension negotiations is essential. The General and Municipal Workers Union policy, for example, is to seek good pension schemes without putting jobs at risk and not to insist that every scheme must immediately comply with every aspect of the union's objectives before it is recommended to the members. The union does insist that pensions are negotiable and that the members are fully involved.

This means, for instance, that where a scheme is considerably underfunded the union's negotiators will give first priority to achieving an adequate level of funding. In some cases this could well mean contemplating an increase in the member's contribution although one would normally expect any deficit to be met by the employer. A recent example of the responsible approach was with a medium-sized fund operated by the British subsidiary of a multi-national company. The shop stewards at local level had been seeking substantial improvements in the works pension scheme; examination of the actuarial valuation, however, showed a deficiency of several million pounds and a statement by the Actuary that "at the age where most people transferred the overall contribution rate is not sufficient to provide the future service element of the benefits". Faced with this situation the union's Pensions Officer advised the shop stewards:

"Although my general conclusion will be of immediate disappointment with the improvement aspirations that I naturally share with you and your colleagues, I must emphasise even more strongly than before, the first priority must be to deal with the valuation deficiencies and to secure some increase in the Company's normal level of funding.

"I consider it imperative that you communicate this priority to the Company at your forthcoming meeting, as in my view we would not be acting in a responsible manner if we attempted to improve the existing benefits before the Company takes action to correct the present unsatisfactory funding situation."

Perhaps this does not illustrate the usual attitude that the commentators expect from trade unions, but there can be no point in attempting to negotiate expensive promises that cannot be kept.

COLLECTIVE BARGAINING

A relevant issue is the position to be given to pensions in the total wage package. The common riposte by management to the statement that "pensions are deferred pay" is to ask whether the scheme members will forego part of their pay rise towards the cost of improvements. The trade unions would reply that the question must be taken in its context. If a claim including pensions is submitted as a "package" it should be dealt with accordingly. No one would deny the difficulties, especially as the time scale for negotiating pensions can be very different from that for negotiating a wage claim. Ideally there must be general acceptance of the idea of a "trade off" in some sense—a principle not readily accepted by those who in the past have been subjected to paternalistic managements.

PAY CODE

On the other hand, during periods of pay restraint, employees cannot be expected to agree very readily to new or increased pension contributions. The phased return to free collective bargaining must include the proper planning of pensions with full costs revealed and disparities eliminated. The 1975/6 and 1976/7 pay policies (the Labour Government/TUC Social Contract) brought pensions under the guidelines*. Pension improvements were permitted, however, up to a minimum contracting-out level in preparation for April 1978. For a great many manual workers trapped in inadequate money purchase schemes the exemption gave an enormous area for improvement.

Press comment on the seamen's dispute in September 1976 carried the implication that the TUC were somehow "evading" the pay policy by pointing out to the seamen the *permitted* exceptions such as pensions and sick-pay improvements. The unions neither shared nor understood this attitude. There had been overwhelming evidence of the union's commitment to the pay guidelines. But they were restrictive and they did call for sacrifice by their members. Where, therefore, for good reasons, exceptions were made, they saw no reason not to take advantage of them.

THE MODEL SCHEME?

What then is the model scheme which the unions seek to achieve?

How near do they come to reaching their aspiration?

Evidence on the quality of pension schemes as a whole is limited and generally out of date. The Government Actuary Department's (GAD) last survey was in 1971 and a further survey is currently in progress. Sample surveys such as the GMWU's own study and that undertaken by the National Association of Pension Funds are "snapshots" and will include schemes that have recently been improved or introduced, schemes that have never been improved, and schemes where active discussions upon improvements are in train. This chapter therefore seeks to compare the aspirations of trade union members with the available statistical evidence as a whole but to take an impressionistic rather than a statistical view of the success or failure of these aspirations.

*As from 1.8.77 pensions were freed from constraint.

Comment must be made upon the various surveys used for this purpose. The GAD 1971 survey was the fourth—previous surveys were made in 1956, 1963, and 1967. It was based on a sample of 3000 companies selected from the National Insurance records of 1 in 9000 employees. It is the only survey that can really claim to be statistically sound, and were it not 6 years out of date could be used by itself. (It is appropriate here to put in a plea that economic and manpower considerations are not allowed to cause another lengthy gap between surveys; the lack of up-dated adequate information ultimately becomes self-defeating.)

The NAPF survey (1975)* is the first of an intended annual series. All member schemes were invited to complete a detailed questionnaire, but the response rate was only 42%. Any bias is probably towards the larger, better-informed, and more alert scheme managements.

The GMWU survey makes no claims to be representative; it is the analysis of 122 of the more than 300 schemes with which the Head Office Pensions and Social Services Department had been involved between January 1974 and November 1975. The selection of the schemes is a random one, although the basis of selection has probably biased the sample somewhat towards smaller schemes where the Department had only reported upon them rather than those where it had taken an active part in the negotiations. However, given that it is a 1 in 3 sample, any sampling error is unlikely to be large.

In the nature of things, the cross-section of schemes examined was not a representative sample of all schemes. They come from the employers (still too few) who recognise pensions as a matter for negotiation/consultation, and from firms where the union organisation is reasonably strong. The vast majority of such schemes are either designed specifically for manual workers or with manual workers included on an equal footing with staff.

Finally, in many cases the schemes were either established or suitably amended prior to the survey, in some cases to conform

*Since the compilation of this typescript the NAPF have issued a second survey details of which are obtainable from the National Association of Pension Funds, Prudential House, Wellesley Road, Croydon, CR0 2AD.

with the 1973 Social Security Act recognition requirements, in others since their abandonment with the Better Pensions anticipated "contracted-out" conditions in mind. Some, however, are much older schemes up to 15 or 20 years old, on which the Department may have been asked to comment with a view to negotiation of possible changes; negotiations may not have been successful or may not have been concluded. The sample, therefore, was not a "snapshot" of the schemes with which the Department was dealing at the time but a cross-section of those that had been dealt with since the Department was established in January 1974.

It is interesting to note the result of a separate investigation which was carried out at the same time as this survey but for a different purpose. It was to ascertain how many schemes the GMWU were actively involved in negotiating after May 1974 when Mrs. Barbara Castle announced the abandonment of the State Reserve Scheme until November 1975. That investigation showed that 112 schemes had been involved, covering somewhere between 1¼ and 1½ million workers. That sampling clearly overlaps somewhat with the survey sample, but not entirely because of the different method of selection.

Often even good schemes are poor at communicating the fact that they *are* good to their members. The GMWU took its information on schemes from the documents available to ordinary scheme members, sometimes amplified by information obtained during negotiations. In practice, schemes can be more generously administered than the rules would suggest; but it is the rules as conveyed to members that are of prime importance.

Taking the foregoing into account, the statistics in the union's survey are probably reliable enough to be used for discussions of trends but not in terms of exact percentages.

THE ASPIRATIONS AND THE RESULT

MEMBERSHIP

The unions seek that pension schemes should be open to all employees (male and female) either on joining the Company or after a reasonable waiting period (probably not more than a year). There are varying opinions on the age at which young people should be brought into a scheme. On the one hand, teenage marriage is fairly commonplace and it is not unusual for an 18 year old to be married and have dependants. In addition, with an entry age later than 20 it is impossible for women to complete their full 40 years in a scheme due to their earlier retirement age, but the average 18 year old is not particularly interested in pensions and strongly resents an extra deduction from the pay packet. A sensible compromise can be reached by the provision of a lower entry age of 20 but extending the death-in-service lump-sum benefit on a non-contributory basis to those between 18 and 20 years of age. The cost for such young employees is negligible.

At the upper end, schemes should be open to all those within a year of retirement. This point will assume greater importance as the preservation requirements of the Social Security Act 1973 begin to take effect. Late entrants to an employment who have accrued pension rights with other employers will wish to enter pension schemes and earn pension rights up to normal retirement age so that the aggregate of their pension entitlements will be reasonable related to their earning capacity on retirement. Furthermore, such older entrants to employment should not be denied cover against death in service.

The GAD survey in 1971 found that the majority of schemes impose a minimum age for entry. In the private sector there was a lower proportion than before of women members in schemes with no minimum age but the reduction was not very great. By comparing the "schemes" and "members" totals in the survey it could be inferred that on average the larger the scheme the less restrictions on the conditions of entry, especially for women. In the public sector the minimum age for entry is usually less than 21.

In commenting upon maximum age limits for entry the survey said:

> "As the retirement age is usually 65 for men and 60 for women it appears that by setting this requirement, many employers

implicitly impose a minimum of 5 or 10 years service for the grant of normal pension on age grounds. However, about 10% of schemes covering 20% of scheme members have an explicit requirement of a minimum period of service within the scheme as a condition for the award of an age retirement pension. In the public sector entry is, in the majority of cases, permitted right up to retiring age, but a minimum of 10 years service within the scheme is usually required; this qualifying period was reduced to 5 years in public service schemes while the enquiry was in progress, and the remainder of the public sector may well follow suit.''

The NAPF Survey did not cover this feature, but the GMWU survey found the area showing a considerable diversity of treatment: from the 122 schemes 57 different variations were found. The most common was male 21–64, female 21–59 with 15 (12%) cases, examples of other types being:

(a) Male 20–50, female 20–45, with management discretion beyond that age—one case.
(b) Male 24–55, females excluded—one case.
(c) Male 21–60, female 30–50.

In all, 71 of the schemes (58%) surveyed had entry ages that were unsatisfactory because of either a restrictive lower age limit or a restrictive upper age limit or both on all employees or on female employees. Of those schemes that did not overtly exclude women, 27 (10%) had lower age limits which were higher for women than for men. In 49 cases (40%) the upper age of entry was 5 years or more before retiring age for men or women or both. This I would regard as unsatisfactory because it means an employee changing his job at a late stage cannot earn a pension related to his salary at retirement.

QUALIFICATION PERIODS

Qualification periods should not normally be longer than a year. This is long enough to cope with the situation of an employer who relies heavily on student or seasonal labour, but any longer period will seriously reduce an employee's pensionable service. Management will frequently argue against this, claiming that labour turnover is high over longer periods of years, but the unions would tend to take the view that it is the labour practices that should be changed rather than the pension scheme eligibility.

The Government Actuary found that a qualifying period of service, although common in the private sector, is somewhat less so than a minimum age requirement as with the minimum age condition; the imposition of less severe requirements appears to be associated with a larger size of scheme. In the public sector, qualifying service is required only in a minority of cases.

An analysis of private sector schemes jointly by minimum age and the minimum service qualifications for entry showed that an age requirement was often found on its own without any service requirement, but that it was rare to find qualifying service required where there was no age test. A wide diversity of combinations was found in cases where both types of condition were imposed. Short qualifying periods and a low minimum age were associated to a moderate degree, but it did not appear that the two types of test are generally used as alternatives.

The GMWU found that in a number of cases the qualification period was not stated. In those where it was, the most usual period was 1 year's service with 25 cases. In total, 35 cases (29%) had qualification periods for all staff of 1 year or less. The maximum found was 10 years in one case. Twelve schemes asked a longer qualification period for women than men (often in addition to a later entry age), and one had a 1-year qualification period for staff, 5 years for works. In 14 cases (11%) coverage for lump-sum death-in-service benefit was available from an earlier date than pensions coverage—on the first day of entry, at an earlier age, or immediately on attaining the qualifying age, when the pension scheme had a single annual entry date. These figures show a very substantial measure of discrimination against women, which will have to be eliminated to comply with the equal access requirements of the Social Security Act 1975. The Act provides that men and women must be admitted to pension schemes on terms which are the same as to the age and length of service required for admission and whether the scheme be voluntary or obligatory.

THE OCCUPATIONAL PENSIONS BOARD AND THE "EQUAL ACCESS" REQUIREMENTS

Where an employer does not comply with these requirements the OPB can order back-service funding by the employer for up to 2 years. The Act also provides that in deciding to contract in or out the employer must not discriminate except in terms of category of employment. There are obvious loopholes here in that there is, as yet, no legislation enforcing equal *status* within schemes, and employers will be able to discriminate against "categories of employment" which happen to contain mainly women. A tendency is appearing for employers to level down rather than up pensions, i.e. to increase the male minimum entry age or qualification period rather than lower the female, or to make the male scheme voluntary rather than the female compulsory. This tendency is being resisted by the unions.

It is often said that women do not want to join pension schemes or pay a full contribution. Obviously the genuine implementation of equal pay is changing this as women begin to achieve earnings from which it is reasonable to expect deductions to be made for a pension. The average woman's consciousness of pensions is also greatly heightened; fewer women now want to be treated merely as their husband's dependant in retirement. Possibly Sir Keith Joseph's Act did women an unrecognised service in 1973 because the blatant discrimination against them, inherent in the State Reserve Scheme, first alerted many women to the whole question of equality in pension schemes.

Feedback from the shop stewards and delegates at conferences, the interest the OPB report has aroused, the take up by women in schemes where they have recently been offered membership all point to the fact that women *are* interested. Those managements who are still saying "it would be very unpopular if we were to ask our women workers to pay full contributions" might actually try asking them, with all the provisos about proper communication of benefits that have already been made. They might be surprised.

In any case, in the future, with the Social Security Pensions Act and the phasing out of the married women's option, the choice for men and women will become much more equal. There will remain, of course, the great stumbling block of unequal retirement ages, but there is unlikely to be a change in the foreseeable future because of the cost (£2000 million being the approximate cost in November 1976 terms to reduce the male retirement age to 60).

Sanctions on difficult employers are available both through the industrial tribunals and through the procedure for obtaining a certificate for contracting out. As the Trico–Folberth pay case in 1976 showed, of course, industrial tribunals can take a very narrow view, but equally the case has shown that women are willing to take prolonged industrial action to enforce their rights.

The issue is an important one because the "growth area" in scheme membership must largely be among women. In 1971 only 500,000 women in manual work in the private sector were members.

Over the last 20 years the rise in the numbers in the labour force (the "economically active") has been entirely due to an increase in the proportion of women going out to work. While the percentage of economically active men dropped from 88% to 81% between 1951 and 1971, for women the proportion of economically active has risen from 35% to 43%. This means that whereas once a woman's working life could be seen as marginal, both to her life cycle as a whole, and to the economy, now it has to be recognised that for most women their life pattern will in the future be one of considerable periods of work interrupted by short periods of child bearing, and this changed pattern must be catered for in pension scheme design.

VOLUNTARY OR COMPULSORY MEMBERSHIP?

So far as schemes being voluntary or compulsory is concerned, membership of a good scheme which has been negotiated with the unions is normally acceptable as a condition of employment. Experience has shown that in a voluntary scheme the recommendation of the unions for their members to join can greatly influence the acceptance rate.

The GAD survey did not cover the question of whether membership of a scheme was voluntary or compulsory. The NAPF survey did cover this point and found that membership was as Table 1 shows.

TABLE 1

	Staff schemes		Works schemes		Combined schemes		All schemes	
	Males (%)	Females (%)	Males (%)	Females (%)	Males (%)	Females (%)	Males (%)	Females (%)
Voluntary	6	23	29	30	16	24	14	24
Compulsory	93	74	69	56	83	74	85	71
Not applicable	1	3	2	14	1	2	1	5

Source: NAPF Survey of Occupational Pension Schemes, 1975.

Table 1 reveals the expected differences in the conditions of entry for males and females with 93% of staff schemes making membership compulsory for males whilst the corresponding figure for females is only 74%. It is interesting to note that although the figures for females in staff and combined schemes are of the same order, there is a drop in the number of combined schemes which make membership for males obligatory.

It was found that the size of scheme membership had an influence in so far as the smaller schemes were more likely to allow voluntary membership. This characteristic was most clearly displayed in works schemes where only 44% of schemes with under 100 members made membership compulsory for males (corresponding figure for females was 33%) whilst the figure for works schemes with over 10,000 members was 95% (82% for females).

The majority of schemes included under "not applicable" are almost certainly those which relate to companies whose nature of business precludes the use of female employees.

The GMWU survey showed that of the 122 pension schemes surveyed 36 (30%) were open to all grades, 12 (10%) were restricted to staff, and 24 (20%) were restricted to "works", "manual", or "hourly paid" employees; 2 were not known. In 5 cases employees had to be on some sort of register before joining—a register of "permanent" or "pensionable" employees. In 11 cases females were specifically excluded, and in 1 case females were eligible only if single. However, 2 out of the 11 cases were in industries where few, if any, females are employed. In 33 cases (27%) membership was stated to be a condition of employment for the grades included, but there may be other cases in which it is in the contract of employment but not in the scheme booklet. In a small number of cases membership was compulsory for men, voluntary for women, or voluntary for women up to a particular age or service level. Membership of one scheme was a condition of service for staff employees, voluntary for women. In 28 cases (23%) membership was restricted to "whole-time" or "full-time" employees. In a number of other cases a minimum number of hours' work was specified.

There is no reason to suppose that the proportion of part-time employees in the economy is going to fall in the future; indeed, it may well rise. It would be grossly unfair if they were consigned automatically to the State scheme without the possibility of even augmented benefits. Restrictions on part-time employees should be reduced or abolished. Certainly all employees working sufficient hours to be covered by the Employment Protection Act should be admitted to schemes, including women working short hours but who are long-service employees. The Employment Protection Act extends protection to those working 16 hours or more a week or those with 5 years of service who work at least 8 hours a week.

From the union standpoint a fair amount of negotiating success has been gained on improving the ages of entry with less success recorded on qualification periods. Few employers have been willing to go the whole way on part-time employment.

There have been some novel arrangements where an employer has been willing to concede on one or two items but not on others. In one case of a voluntary scheme with a 3-year qualification period, for example, the employer has extended the death-in-service benefits to those not yet qualified, but the benefit is withdrawn if the employee does not join the scheme at the first opportunity. Moreover, employees joining over the age of 62 (male) and 57 (female) will be offered special death cover on production of medical evidence after a 3-month waiting period.

NORMAL RETIREMENT DATE

Pressure for the reduction of the State retirement age for men has come largely from manual workers' unions. In occupational schemes it is in general only an aspiration outside the public sector, though common in "top hat" schemes. The Government Actuary found the following result across the board—it is a pity he did not separate his findings into manual and non-manual:

"In the great majority of cases in the private sector, pension ages follow the National Insurance standard of 65 for men and 60 for women. Retirement for women at 65 is now rarer than was found in the 1963 enquiry, when this feature was found in 10% of schemes. An appreciable proportion of both sexes retire at younger ages than standard, although these are in a relatively small number of schemes. In the public sector age 60 is a much more common pension age for men than in the private sector. There is also an appreciable number of men who can retire between age 60 and 65 on completion of a certain period of service."

The NAPF commented that the overwhelming majority of occupational pension schemes adhere to the standard State retirement ages of 65 for men and 60 for women. It would seem, however, that for men the works schemes adhere to this standard more closely than do the staff or combined schemes.

While the GMWU found too few schemes with a retirement date other than 65 and 60 to be worth commenting upon, there is some evidence in fact that schemes which previously had a common retirement date of, say, 62 have turned towards the majority pattern.

The GMWU's longer term objective is for a full (two-thirds) pension after 35 years of service payable at age 60 for all. Unless the State pension age is reduced or made flexible, however, the objective is generally unattainable. In fact in some circumstances it could be unsatisfactory since unless the pension is at a generous level it will do little more than debar the individual from supplementary benefit.

In view of the high cost of funding pensions for males at age 60, although highly desirable, in my view this aspiration should receive lower priority than seeking to improve the level of benefits. Should the benefits from the occupational scheme be at or near maximum approvable limits, then of course the possibility becomes greater. Even then provision must be made for financially "bridging the gap" until the State pension becomes payable.

CONTRIBUTIONS

Depending on the precise "package" of benefits and the age, wage, and service distributions of the workforce, the cost of a 60ths scheme with a generous range of other benefits is unlikely to cost less than 15% of the pay roll. (If the costs of benefits is assessed on a cautious basis allowing for only a small long-term real return on investment, i.e. in accordance with current actuarial practice, the minimum of 15% is rather on the low side.) Ideally, this should be paid entirely by the employer, but obviously in most cases for historical reasons this is simply unrealisable. The employer should certainly contribute on a ratio of not less than twice the employees' rate.

Table 2 from the GAD survey shows the proportions of private sector schemes which have various types of members' contributions or are non-contributory (i.e. the member makes no payment for retirement benefits). It shows a trend in the private sector towards assessing contributions as a percentage of salary. The same trend was noted in the previous review and is doubtless associated with a movement towards the salary service type of pension benefit.

TABLE 2. TYPES OF MEMBERS' CONTRIBUTIONS: PRIVATE SECTOR

	Proportions of schemes	
	1967 (%)	1971 (%)
Percentage of salary	25	34
Dependent on salary range	20	20
Flat	20	9
Other basis	5	2
All contributory schemes	70	65
Non-contributory schemes	30	35
Total	100	100

Turning now to the basis of members' contributions, the NAPF survey quoted the information given in Table 3.

TABLE 3

	Staff schemes (%)	Works schemes (%)	Combined schemes (%)	All schemes (%)
Contributory schemes				
Flat amount	3	20	5	7
Dependent on salary	76	55	77	72
Total	79	75	82	79
Non-contributory schemes	21	25	18	21

Source: NAPF Survey of Occupational Pension Scheme, 1975.

The most significant feature is that whilst 20% of works used the flat contribution basis it was no longer fashionable amongst staff and combined schemes.

The GMWU survey dealing with contributions said that perhaps the most striking point is the number of variations both in the rates and in the way they were expressed. For employers' contributions, 38 variations in a sample of 122 were counted (not including differences in wording); for employees 34. Probably the single most common scheme is where the employee pays 5% or thereabouts and the employer the balance of the cost, but there are many others.

It is impossible to give a fair assessment of contribution rates because of the reticence of employers on this point, more particularly on their own contributions. (In a very small percentage of cases, 2 out of the total sample, not even the employee's rate is given in the scheme booklet.) But in 25 out of the 122 schemes studied, no information at all was given. In another 14 cases some idea was given, but only in the vaguest possible terms: "the company's contribution will more than match the employee's" ... "will be considerably in excess" ... "is always more...". A number of companies seemed to regard this as an opportunity for point-scoring rather than imparting information, which in my view is mistaken. Some of the least informative schemes, in fact, were ones where the Company must really have been paying quite heavily. Of the 7 non-contributory ones, for instance, only 1 stated specifically how much the employer was paying for it. Two others stated simply that they were paying "the whole cost", and the other 4 gave no information.

Of the other 83 schemes which did give some information, 42 only stated that the employer was paying "the balance of the cost" or the balance plus the whole cost of some component such as life assurance. Where an employer is guaranteeing a scheme it is possible that he feels that to give a particular rate for his contribution would be misleading because it might change. But it is unlikely to change much between valuations, and there is everything to be said in terms of good industrial relations for giving members a clear idea of their *actual* benefits.

Of the 39 that gave a clearer idea (32%), 20 gave it in exact percentage terms. These ranged from 2½% to 9.2% with the majority in the range of 7–8½%. The exception was a non-contributory scheme with an employer's rate of 15%. The remainder used some less-precise term, such as "about twice", "2½ times", "more than two-thirds" or "more than 60%", and there is also included in this total one flat-rate scheme where the employer pays in 10p for every 10p put in by the workers.

Only one scheme specified that the employer paid in different contributions for men and women. Since it is known that many others do this, one could speculate on the reasons for this reticence.

Not surprisingly, employers gave a good deal more information to employees about their contributions. The main findings are summarised in Table 4.

TABLE 4

	No.	%
Under 3%	28	23
3% and under 5%	34	28
5% and over	37	31
Flat rate	8	6
Non-contributory	8	6
Various other	7	6
Total	122	100

(Where a two-tier scheme is involved the scheme has been taken as falling within the lower tier.)

Some qualifications need to be made to these figures. First, where a scheme adopts integration of its contribution rate it is often not easy to disentangle from the booklet just how much of the total contribution rate is going to the occupational benefit. Second, because these are percentages of different things, i.e. depending on what items are included in pensionable pay, so someone paying 3% of PAYE earnings may, in fact, be paying as much as someone paying 5% or 6% of basic.

These figures can be compared with the GAD survey for 1971: some caution is needed because this survey was so much larger and was based on replies to a questionnaire rather than scheme booklets, but the comparison is nonetheless valid.

Their figures are compared in Table 5.

TABLE 5

	GAD manual	GMWU
Under 3%	60	29
3% and under 5%	34	34
5% and over	6	37
Total	100	100

The differences, in all probability, are due to improved schemes being negotiated during the period subject to survey.

It must be said that in a number of cases scheme booklets are extremely unclear about the contribution rate, even to the extent of not giving the employee's rate.

The marked reluctance of certain employers to reveal their costs tends to breed intense distrust on the part of their employees—a certain "contribution" to unsatisfactory relationships.

Where a scheme negotiation has been sensibly carried out, the question hardly arises because the unions will have been provided with copies of the actuarial advice from the outset. The issue of "opening the books" on pension schemes is an emotive one, but its importance cannot be over-stressed. It has been suggested that the request from a union to have sight of an actuarial report casts doubt on the accuracy of the professional opinion. I contend that such professional advice should be available to both sides to assist in the mutual determination of the decision to be taken.

TYPE OF SCHEME

All studies show an increasing trend towards final earnings schemes, the trend which the Government Actuary pointed to in 1971. The NAPF 1975 survey showed a further development in the trend, whilst emphasising the gap between staff and works schemes (Table 6).

TABLE 6. NORMAL RETIREMENT BENEFIT BASIS

Basis	Staff schemes (%)	Works schemes (%)	Combined schemes (%)	All schemes (%)	Staff and combined schemes (%)
Final or final average salary	99	54	95	88	97
Career average salary	1	16	2	4	1
Salary grade	—	2	3	2	1
Flat rate	—	27	—	6	—

Source: NAPF Survey of Occupational Pension Schemes, 1975.

The NAPF survey showed that 29% of works and 45% of staff schemes were integrated with State benefits; the GAD dealt with it briefly, finding an integration disregard in 20% of schemes. The GMWU found a level of integrated schemes between the two (24%). The differences are partly because some of the GAD "other" schemes will be integrated, partly because a higher level of State pension and the need for higher contributions are making an offset increasingly popular, especially with a good level of pension accrual.

Out of the 29 schemes that were "integrated" by including a State pension offset on pensionable earnings, just over half had this in terms such as "1½ times State pension" or had an automatic regulation in their rules for changing the offset when the pension changed. In the rest it was stated as a fixed sum, which was rapidly being rendered irrelevant by inflation. One scheme, for instance, had £200 offset, others £390, £400, £520, or £603.

Trade unions are, in general, opposed to any system of integration of occupational schemes with State benefits; the TUC, for instance, say: "It is only worthwhile making an adjustment for Social Security benefits if maximum scheme benefits are likely to be obtained, because otherwise they provide a convenient way of providing the lower earners with proportionately higher benefits. Also there are practical and psychological objections to making adjustments for such benefits."

Nevertheless, it is recognised by union negotiators that the cost of providing pensions is increasing; integration is one way of reducing the cost to both employer and employees. The "fair and just" test of any integration formula must be to ensure that the ultimate target benefit is adequate.

The GMWU survey revealed the following pattern of types of schemes (the fact that the total membership of the schemes covered by the survey was in excess of 1 million being more significant than the actual number of schemes involved). In the large majority of the schemes the pension was based either on final salary or on final salary integrated with the State pension. Table 7 shows the numbers in each category.

In all, 81% of schemes were final salary, the remainder being of

TABLE 7

Type of scheme	No.	%
Integrated final	29	24.0
Final	69	57.0
Average	9	7.0
Money purchase	11	9.0
Graded average	4	3.0
Total	122	100.0

little use in an inflationary period, i.e. average salary, money purchase, and flat rate.

This contrasts markedly with the GAD survey of 1971 which found only 55% of schemes to be based on final salary. It is, no doubt, a reflection of the fact that very many of our schemes are of recent origin or modification, when the onset of inflation was making other types of scheme progressively less suitable. But it also contrasts with the NAPF survey and serves to again underline the gap that must be closed before manual equality with staff benefits is reached.

The contracting-out consultations under the Pensions Act initially and in the future should serve to meet this end.

ACCRUAL RATE

Table 8 shows the Government Actuary's findings for final salary schemes.

TABLE 8

	Proportion of schemes		Proportion of members	
	Staff schemes (%)	Manual schemes (%)	Staff schemes (%)	Manual schemes (%)
Less than 80ths	6	74	3	74
80ths	24	18	22	7
Between 80ths and 60ths	11	3	8	15
60ths or better	59	5	67	4
Total	100	100	100	100

The NAPF survey found an improved position for both staff and manual schemes, and the GMWU survey gives a more satisfactory picture, too, probably due again to negotiating success with hourly paid (manual or works) schemes.

For future service under the scheme accrual rates varied widely, but the most common were 60ths and 80ths integrated (23% in both cases); 100ths came next in importance with 12.3%, but there were a large number of other variations ranging from 130ths down to 44ths. There were also a number variable according to age or grade, and a number of two-tier schemes. Table 9 gives details.

TABLE 9

Accrual rate	% of schemes
Better than 60ths	4.1
60ths	23.0
Between 60ths and 80ths	5.7
80ths	23.0
100ths and over	13.1
Two-tier	4.9
Integrated 60ths	7.3
Other	18.9
Total	100.0

Clearly a 60ths scheme which gives a two-thirds pension on retirement is the common aim. An 80ths scheme on *all* earnings and *all* service will provide a higher pension than the State scheme but is still below the unions' best aspirations.

Where a scheme defines pensionable salary as "total earnings" and there is no deductive item, the minimum accrual rate for contracting out is 100ths (1%). That is to say the Occupational Pensions Board have ruled that this is the equivalent of 80ths with a deductive item of one and a half times the lower earnings limit subject to the normal guaranteed minimum pension calculation.

It is most likely that the unions would resist contracting out on a 100ths basis unless the employer had agreed to negotiate further improvements as financial or other circumstances allowed.

PAST SERVICE

Generally, adequate treatment of past service in previous schemes tends to be more important probably for manual workers than for white collar workers. (White collar workers are unlikely to have been consigned for years to schemes offering flat-rate benefits shredded in value by inflation.) There is a need for generous back-service crediting for these members, this being the only really practicable way of inflation proofing their benefits at least to retirement age. The reluctance to follow this path is, of course, on the grounds of cost.

An older employee brought into a reasonable scheme towards the end of his service does not really appreciate contributing to a miniscule pension. The problem is immensely complicated, particularly in the large conglomerates which resulted from the merger mania of the sixties.

In some cases where there has been a satisfactorily negotiated scheme to take care of future service there are pockets of considerable discontent due to inadequate past-service rights. Unless this potential problem area receives proper care and priority attention, one can foresee industrial muscle playing a prominent part in extracting past service rights. If the concept of pensions being deferred pay is accepted totally, then those closest to retirement age might well be able to produce a convincing case that they have been deprived of their deferred pay in the past—particularly during the several periods of "immediate pay" restraint suffered during their working lifetime.

PENSIONABLE SALARY

It is a cliché to say that earnings structures differ between staff and manual workers; they differ far more on that basis, in fact, right across industry than they do as a result of negotiation between different industries. Typically, a staff worker will get 90% or more of his earnings from basic salary. Manual workers, however, get only

70% of their earnings from this source: the rest comes from overtime, piece work, and "payments by results" systems of one sort or
another. There are several industries in fact where the "basic wage"
is a purely nominal figure on the shop floor, simply a calculator used
to work out earnings or give a guarantee. A manual worker's
earnings, therefore, are far more liable to fluctuation, and typically
tend to fall in the last few years of his working life as performance
decreases with age, whereas the earnings of general management
peak at the end of their working lives.

A scheme that provides pensions throughout a company on the
basis of pensionable earnings being basic wages/salary and final
pensionable earnings being the final year's or even the final 3 years'
basic wages/salary averages, while it looks superficially equal for all,
is in fact giving a worse deal to the manual workers than to management because the pension will be calculated on a smaller proportion
of their take-home pay and on earnings *after* they have peaked, but a
scheme calculated on PAYE earnings and either the final year or the
best 3 years in the last 13 *revalued,* as the Inland Revenue allows, is
giving an equal deal to everyone. On the calculation of final pensionable pay the GAD's results are shown in Table 10.

TABLE 10. AVERAGING FORMULA FOR SALARY IN SALARY SERVICE SCHEMES

Salary on which pension is based	Proportions of schemes	Proportions of members	
	Private sector (%)	Private sector (%)	Both sectors (%)
Final pay	8	20	12
Average of last 1 year's pay	12	11	8
Average of last 3 years' pay	29	38	62
Average of last 5 years' pay	20	22	13
Pay 5 years before normal pension age	26	6	3
Other	5	3	2
Total	100	100	100

The NAPF's results were rather different, and point to the increasing popularity of the ''best 3 in 10'' formula, and the near disappearance of the ''5 years before pension age'' rule, presumably because of the effects of inflation.

The GMWU's survey found that out of the total of 98 schemes (69 final, 29 integrated) 52 calculated final pensionable earnings on average pensionable remuneration for the best 3 years out of the last 10. A further 11 calculated on the last 3 years and 3 gave option of the last 3 or best 3 in the last 10. Given current inflation, these variations will, in fact, all come down to the last 3 years (usually tax years, but occasionally ''scheme'' years) and thus 66, or just over two-thirds, calculated in this way.

It must be realised that this sort of modification can mean a serious shortfall in income from a scheme which seeks to provide two-thirds of final earnings given the inflation we are currently experiencing. One wonders whether it is generally realised that there is provision in the Inland Revenue Superannuation Funds Office Practice Notes for the use of a revaluation factor in the calculation of final remuneration for pension purposes, so that each year's actual earnings could be increased by an allowance to allow for inflation.

The variety of definitions of pensionable earnings was illustrated in this form by the GMWU. In 55% of schemes surveyed calculation of contributions and pension was, or appeared to be, based on PAYE earnings (appeared to be in the sense that there were some cases in which the definition of earnings was not clear, but there was nothing to contradict the assumption of total earnings). Table 11 shows the types of definitions used:

TABLE 11

Pensionable earnings	No.	%
PAYE	67	55
Basic + some other components	25	20
Basic only	19	16
Fixed weekly contribution	7	6
Not clear from booklet	4	3
Total	122	100

For staff and manual workers, PAYE is usually the preferred definition. Management may argue that manual workers' earnings fluctuate too wildly and that their use may penalise the older worker who cannot undertake so much overtime. However, it is the unions' view that a pension should reflect the individual's standard of living, and PAYE is thought to be the best yardstick upon which to calculate the pension.

In the calculation of final pensionable earnings the manual worker whose earnings capacity may fall off well before retirement can be provided for (a) through a special formula going to earnings outside the last 13 years (the Inland Revenue have approved one for a large scheme negotiated by the unions), (b) through the permitted indexing of earnings within the last 10 years, or (c) by breaking away from final earnings altogether and using revalued average earnings instead.

COMMUTATION

The facility to commute all or part of one's pension is valued by a great many pension scheme members. It is, however, one that must not be "over sold" in a contracted-out scheme because the need to retain the guaranteed minimum pension uncommuted will impose severe restrictions on the amount of lump sum available.

Obviously members should have the right to commute to the maximum permissible by law. A clear explanation of possible limitations must be given at the outset to avoid disappointment and associated frustrations at retirement.

A particular point that needs to be looked at is the question of commutation of trivial amounts. Figures provided by the Department of Health and Social Security show that in 1973 nearly half the occupational pensions in payment were under £6, which compares with the Supplementary Benefit occupational pension disregard of £1 plus average housing costs per household in that year of £5.43. In other words a great many people taking a pension can find themselves caught in what has been called the "poverty pinch" where their occupational pension simply disqualifies them from receiving supplementary benefit without making them any better off. For many people, particularly in view of increased disregard of savings, commutation of the whole of a small pension can be the most sensible move, and it is urgently necessary that schemes, particularly older schemes, should allow it.

The Government Actuary found that the right to commute part of the pension was to be found in about 30% of private sector schemes, covering the same proportions of members, and being most common in salary/service type schemes.

Only a very small proportion of private sector members are accruing rights to an unconditional lump sum at retirement, although this is common in the public sector. For both sectors combined lump-sum retirement benefits will be available to 50% of all scheme members, and the exercise of a commutation option will be required for only two-fifths of this group.

The NAPF survey result reflected that works schemes are less likely (39%) to provide members with the option to commute their pensions for a lump sum (17% in all schemes).

An investigation into the possible effect of the method of investment on the commutation provision revealed that "insured" and "managed" fund schemes are more likely to provide lump-sum option than privately invested schemes. This correlation was found to be more apparent in staff and combined schemes than in works schemes.

The GMWU survey showed that 39 (32%) of the schemes in the sample specified that they allowed commutation "within revenue limits" and 2 of these also said that they allowed commutation of the whole pension on grounds of serious ill health. A further 15 permitted up to 3/8ths of salary per year of service, the Inland Revenue maximum under the new code (and 4 of these had a clause allowing increased provision through topping up pension entitlement for late entrants), and 11 permitted commutation of up to a quarter of the pension, which was the Inland Revenue maximum under the old code.

This gives a total of 65 schemes (53%) with commutation at or near the limits. Of the rest 12 had no commutation and 17 may have had but gave no clue in their booklets; 14 stated that commutation was allowed but gave no details. The rest had limited rights—in some cases extremely limited—allowing commutation only where the pension was of a trivial amount or only where there was ill health or a trivial amount, or only if additional voluntary contributions were being made. A specific analysis was not done on the rates of commutation, but it is usual practice to pay £9 per £1 of pension for a man and £11 per £1 of pension for a woman. It is clear, however, that many scheme booklets do not give details of rates, which makes it difficult for a prospective pensioner to make an informed decision on what to do.

This is an issue on which the Occupational Pensions Board's recent report on equal status if carried into legislation will have some effect. The report stated that equal factors for commutation would not be possible until there were equal retirement ages, but that there should be provision for options to be equally available to both sexes. It should be added that there is a strong case for regular reviews of commutation factors to take account of fluctuating interest rates.

EARLY RETIREMENT DUE TO ILL HEALTH

It is regrettable that mortality and morbidity statistics correlate directly with social class. Unskilled workers are more likely to have a limiting long-standing illness than skilled workers who may themselves be more important than managerial workers.

The objective should be that where early retirement at any age is due to permanent ill health or incapacity the member should have the right to retire on an unabated pension, calculated so as to take account of all service, including prospective service to normal retirement date. The Inland Revenue definition of incapacity (meaning physical or mental deterioration which is sufficiently severe to prevent the member from following his normal employment or which may seriously impair earning capacity) adds that it does not mean simply a decline in energy or ability. The fair and correct interpretation of the definition should ensure that malingerers are not allowed to benefit.

There is some evidence that where schemes provide for more generous terms on a discretionary basis it is often interpreted narrowly in practice, more narrowly than the schemes' rules permit. Conversely, it is not uncommon to hear of management who, finding it convenient to ease someone out or to reduce their workforce, offer ill-health retirement spontaneously and unnecessarily. Both extremes are abuses, and should be largely overcome by the appointment of member trustees who are likely to have greater sympathy for their fellow members' difficulties (and perhaps less for those of the Company), but there have also been cases where individuals find it very difficult to be considered by trustees due to the remoteness of administrative functions and discouragement by the ill-informed.

The GAD 1971 survey showed that staff schemes were decidedly better provided for than manual in this area but suggested that there had been distinct improvements since the previous survey in 1967.

The NAPF survey commented that in all but a tiny minority (3%) of schemes there is a provision for an immediate pension to be paid to a member who retires early on the grounds of ill health. It is also apparent that works schemes do not fare badly in this particular aspect of pension practice although it is clear that the method of calculation is generally slightly less liberal than that used in staff or combined schemes. It is, in fact, the latter category of scheme which is most likely to provide ill-health pensions on a generous basis with 25% of schemes calculating the pension by reference to the member's "notional" service.

The GMWU in a 1976 analysis of 200 schemes (i.e. the 122 on the 1975 survey plus 78 more) to provide evidence for the OPB's report on Pensions for the Disabled produced the following information:

   *Actual service actuarially reduced, 45%.
   *Actual service only, 19.5%.
   *Actual and up to half prospective pension, 10.5%.
   *Actual and all prospective service, 6%.

   *Including those where it was at the Company's or the trustees' discretion and/or with service qualification.

Separate disability scheme taking place of early retirement, 4%.
Company discretion only, 2%.
No information given, or only ordinary leaving service entitlement, 13%.

It is possible that some of the least generous schemes in practice augment ill-health pensions. Even taking this into account, however, this analysis provided a gloomy and unsatisfactory outcome. In addition, a number of schemes impose rigid periods of qualifying service: 15 years in 1 case, 10 years in 10 cases, and 5 years in 11 cases.

EARLY RETIREMENT AT THE COMPANY'S REQUEST

Wherever financially possible the maximum pension that the Inland Revenue will approve in these cases should be provided. The cost need not necessarily come out of the scheme: certainly, for instance, in the case of a redundancy of any proportions one would look for a special additional contribution from the employer. It is not generally appreciated that long-term unemployment is directly associated with age, and is a more important determining factor than either region or skill. It is difficult in any region for a man over age 55 to obtain new employment whatever skill he may have, even in times of more "normal" unemployment figures than the present. If he lives in a depressed region or if he has no skill or his skill is obsolete, his difficulties are compounded.

Unemployment benefit is available for one year and then the individual must fall back on supplementary benefit. Because of the structure of the supplementary benefit scheme, he may well find his benefit reduced as a result of receiving an inadequate pension from the Company. In the nature of things, pension scheme administrators are managerial employees, unlikely to be affected personally by these considerations: manual workers are. Recently, for instance, the GMWU was involved in discussions of redundancy terms for a predominantly elderly workforce of a factory in a fairly remote area who had little hope of ever entering employment again. It is likely that without the union's assistance the initial offer of early retirement pensions would have deprived many of supplementary benefits.

The Government Actuary did not deal with early retirement other than on grounds of ill health.

The NAPF survey found that there was unanimity of practice between each class of scheme for both instigated and voluntary retirement.

Table 12 shows the GMWU's survey results.

TABLE 12

	No.	%
Redundancy		
No provision mentioned	84	69
Within 10 years of retirement, accrued pension	6	5
Reduced pension	15	12
Accrued + prospective pension	3	2
As for early leavers	12	10
Other	2	2
Total	122	100
At member's own request		
Within 10 years of NRD* reduced pension	44	36
Over age 50, reduced pension	40	33
Not mentioned	26	22
Qualification period, reduced pension	5	4
Qualification period, normal pension	3	2
Other	4	3
Total	122	100

*Normal Retirement Date.

However, these figures do not tell the whole story as it is known from negotiating experience that in a number of cases redundancy/ early retirement provisions exist outside the scheme itself, with the scheme paying a pension and being reimbursed by the Company. Other companies will negotiate a special agreement for the "one off" situation of large-scale redundancies.

In a number of cases there is an area of company discretion

involved; the "other cases" under redundancy and member's own request include several where payment is entirely at discretion.

Details of the reductions in pension for early retirers are sometimes given but more often not. The scales of reduction where fixed vary a good deal, so that one wonders how much they are soundly based actuarially and how much is guesswork.

It has been rare to achieve anything like the full level of unions' aspirations on early retirement. Companies are extremely wary of writing any sort of commitment into pension scheme rules, perhaps understandably when one realises that redundancies are normally associated with cash flow problems.

Nevertheless, there are occasions when funding of a scheme is unnecessarily fine or "cut to the bone", leaving no scope for assisting those members presented with unwanted early retirement.

In passing it can be said that provision for late retirement tends to be spelt out in considerably more detail in scheme booklets, although almost certainly it affects fewer, particularly manual, workers.

DEATH IN SERVICE

One of the provisions normally most valued by members is the lump-sum death-in-service benefit. The Inland Revenue maximum benefit of four times annual salary plus return of contributions is rarely provided. Clearly the maximum should be the attainable objective on grounds of cost and administrative simplicity. In practice, schemes more often provide twice annual salary which, together with a reasonable level of dependant's pension, must be regarded as acceptable.

Many schemes in the past used a lump sum as an easy substitute for an adequate widow's pension—sometimes providing the two alternatives. This can no longer be the case for contracted-out schemes with the Social Security Pensions Act 1975 enforcing a widow's benefit. It is regrettable to note that there is a trend in some quarters to finance a widow's benefit by cutting back on an existing lump-sum benefit. The unions will surely resist this "penny-pinching" approach for the two elements—the once-for-all sum and the continuing pension are equally important. The objective in this area is that there should be no discrimination between men and women, that there should be a right to a pension for the surviving spouse of a pension scheme member irrespective of sex. The GMWU's own pension scheme has a widower's pension as of right; there are a handful of other schemes providing the entitlement but the spread of this concept has been slow. At the very least one hopes that we shall see an extension of widow's pensions to *dependent* widowers, with trustees' discretion to make payments to another financial dependant if appropriate. Improvement in the lump-sum benefit can provide one of the most frequent snags in the negotiations of a pension scheme. A scheme with a flat-rate benefit of, say, £750 is not uncommon, yet is totally inadequate on any grounds of comparison. It is a simple, inexpensive matter to increase the amount payable to bring it up to a realistic level, but a number of questions must be asked:

- At what date is the improvement to be made?
- Must it await completion of the negotiations or be introduced immediately?
- Is it to be applied to all or only to those opting to join the new (amended) scheme?
- On what earnings and over which period is the sum to be calculated?
- How will the calculation basis fit in with the Company's pay-roll system?

If these seem elementary considerations, experience has proved that the communication and the application of substantially improved death-in-service benefits can be confused. Industrial unrest has followed, and at least one case has been to arbitration, the result being that an award was made on moral grounds due to members' booklets being capable of ambiguous interpretation.

The GAD survey found that in about 5% of private sector cases the benefits paid on the death of a woman or an unmarried man would be lower. On the other hand, some schemes which give widows' pensions on death in service would pay a larger lump sum on a death which did not give rise to a widow's pension. There are a few other cases in which additional payments are made, e.g. for long service, while some schemes provide family income benefits in addition to the basic lump sum. Where the payment is assessed on "other" bases it is usually a multiple of pension which was being provided for by the scheme. But refunds additional to the lump sum are the normal arrangement in the private sector. In general, widows' benefits are found in the larger schemes, and this association is more marked for staff than for manual schemes, thus a considerably greater proportion of staff than manual members are covered for widows' pensions. A widow's pension is usually payable until death or remarriage.

The NAPF commented that staff and combined schemes exhibit very similar characteristics in the provision of death-in-service benefits: 35% of both classes of scheme provide a widow's pension in addition to a lump sum whilst only 2% of schemes gave just the "minimum" benefit of a return of the member's contributions with or without interest.

Works schemes were much less likely to provide widows' pensions on death in service with only 35% of the schemes in this category including such a benefit (as compared to 64% of staff schemes and 63% of combined schemes).

The numbers of schemes providing lump-sum death benefits (apart from a return of the member's contributions) did not vary significantly within each class of scheme, the percentage figures for staff, works, and combined schemes being 89%, 91%, and 87% respectively.

Larger schemes were found to be more likely to provide both lump sums and widows' pensions, the provision of a single benefit being rare amongst schemes with over 5000 members.

The GMWU's findings were that 73 schemes (60%) gave neither a widow's pension nor a dependent children's pension on death in service. A further 20 gave widows' pensions but no children's benefits. Only 5 (4%) allowed a member to nominate a dependant other than a widow, though in two other cases the trustees had discretion. (There may in fact be other cases where either discretion or permitted nomination is included in the rules but not in the scheme booklet.) No scheme in the sample gave an unconditional widower's benefit; 4 gave a benefit for dependent widowers (for other purposes a separate but partly overlapping sample was taken on this point which found 4% dependent widowers' pensions for death in service, none as of right).

The most common type of widow's benefit was a 50% pension, but it varied as to its calculation. Out of 36, 16 of the 50% pensions were on the basis of actual and prospective service, 8 took *some* account of service, and 12 were on the basis of accrued service only. Those that took some account of prospective service tended to calculate on the basis of the pension that would have been provided for the member had he retired through ill health the day before his death, and so were not always very generous.

Of the remaining schemes 2 were salary-based, 2 gave less than 50% of the pension, 2 involved the member giving up some of his rights to a pension himself: the others used a variety of arrangements.

For children's pensions the most common arrangement was that the widow's pension would continue in the event of her death until her youngest child was 18 (10 cases). In 4 of these instances a pension was also payable in the case of a member who was a widower or male divorcé and died leaving children. In one case there was similar provision for children of a family member, and in another it was possible at trustees' discretion. Other arrangements included payment of a dependent child's pension in addition to the widow's pension usually set at a fraction per child. Fractions used varied from 10% to 33%. One scheme gave a pension of one-quarter of the widow's pension to any child of a male member or the dependent child of a female member. Another gave one-sixth of the widow's pension to a child who had one parent surviving, one-third to a child with no parent surviving. There were 19 of these cases. In some of these special provision was made for a child who continued fulltime education after 18 or was incapable of earning his living through handicap.

One point worth noting is the question of the return of members' contributions either with or without interest. Interest was either not payable or else payable at what is now an extremely low rate, 2½% or 3% compound. While it is true that many of the contributions being repaid would have been invested at that rate when originally paid, since then a much higher return will have been obtained and this rate of interest should perhaps be a target for attention in the future.

DEATH AFTER RETIREMENT

Widows' pensions on death after retirement can be provided on an "unconditional" basis, i.e. wherever a deceased pensioner leaves a widow or specified dependant. Alternatively, they can be limited to "allocation" where a member may choose, at or before retirement, to give up part of his pension in exchange for a pension payable to his widow after his death; if a member does not choose to allocate part of his pension in this way there will be no widow's pension. Allocation facilities are not uncommon in schemes which provide an unconditional widow's pension, thus members are enabled, if they wish, to provide for larger widows' benefits or to provide for dependants not covered by the rules.

The GAD findings were as shown in Table 13.

TABLE 13

Type of provision	Private sector		Both sectors
	Schemes (%)	Male members (%)	Male members (%)
Widow's pension: unconditional	10	34	51
allocation only	76	55	41
No provision for widow's pension	14	11	8
Total	100	100	100

A relatively high proportion of manual schemes make no provision for widows. In part this may be because the benefits for some such schemes are at a level which hardly allows scope for allocation. Also a certain number of schemes mainly for manual workers provide only lump sums on retirement, and so the question of benefits on death following retirement does not arise.

The NAPF survey found a very much improved situation (possibly due to the State's proposals since Crossman) including provision for a widow's pension becoming common practice in private schemes. The NAPF's figures were as Table 14 shows.

TABLE 14

Type of provision	Staff schemes (%)	Works schemes (%)	Combined schemes (%)	All schemes (%)
Widow's pension as of right	87	64	85	81
Widow's pension by surrender	10	13	9	10
No widow's benefit provided	3	23	6	8

Source: NAPF Survey of Occupational Pensions, 1975.

The GMWU survey found an even greater prevalence of widows' pensions. Most schemes provide a widow's pension for death after retirement: only 4 in fact made no such provision. The most common pension was 50% of the member's: in all, 96 schemes had this but there was considerable variance in their treatment of benefit immediately after death. In 14 schemes, in the case of a pensioner dying within 5 years of his retirement the balance of his 5 years' pension would be handed over to the widow as a lump sum in addition to her pension; 9 more continued the member's pension at full rate for the remainder of the 5 years after retirement before reducing it to the 50% level. Another scheme gave 6 months' pension (both in addition to a 50% pension) and another gave the return of the members' contributions as a lump sum. There were other levels of pension ranging from 25% to 60% and there were 14 schemes that provided a widow's pension only if the member surrendered part of his. (A number of other schemes also allowed surrender to provide additional widow's pension.)

Only 15 schemes in all provided any sort of widower's pension and only 6 out of these gave it as of right. Of the others, 3 gave it to incapacitated widowers, 1 at the trustees' discretion, and 1 allowed it under the surrender provisions. (The dates of the various schemes span the time at which a widower's pension as of right became acceptable to the Inland Revenue.)

For dependants (which can of course sometimes include widowers) 80 schemes appeared to make no provision, 30 allowed surrender of part of the member's pension to provide for a dependant (whether or not a legal widow existed), and 5 allowed a member to nominate a dependant for a pension of which 3 stated that this could only happen if there was no legal widow. In 5 cases there was trustees' discretion and in 1 of these this could only be exercised if there was no legal widow/widower. One further scheme allowed a male divorcé or widower with a child under 18 to nominate for a dependant's pension; other members had to surrender part of their own pension. A number of schemes in addition allowed that where a member died without leaving a widow within 5 years of retirement, the balance of the pension for those 5 years was payable to his dependants. Schemes may also have had provision for trustees' discretion without including it in their scheme booklet.

Children's pensions for death after retirement came into a different category, but there may have been some overlapping with provision for dependants. It is rare, though not unknown, for a person to have young children still dependent on him after retirement age, and only a small minority of schemes catered for it. In 18 cases the provision was when the widow was dead the pension passed on to dependent children. In a further 9 cases a child's pension was payable in addition to the widow's pension after the member's death. This was usually modelled on the child's pension after death in service.

Of the schemes that provided a widow's or dependant's pension either for death in service or death in retirement, 42 cases reduced this pension for age disparity, 29 stated that a reduction was made for disparity over 10 years, but only 9 of these 29 gave a percentage figure for the reduction per year of difference so that the member could calculate the effect. One scheme reduced for a disparity over 5 years, 5 for over 15 years, the remainder for varying periods between. Altogether there were nine variations in type of reduction—a fact which must again cast some doubt on the actuarial calculations involved and whether again in fact they are simply guesswork. Nine schemes imposed a remarriage bar. Only 2, however, specifically said they did not do so; there may be others in which such a bar is implicit. Ten schemes did not give pensions to the widow of a marriage contracted at or within some period before or after retirement (it is interesting to note that none of the schemes with widower's pensions imposed such a bar).

The GMWU's figures are summarised in Table 15.

TABLE 15

	No.	%
50% widow's pension	96	79
Surrender for widow's pension	14	11
No widow's pension	4	3
Other	8	7
Total	122	100
Widower's pension	15	12
Dependant's pension by surrender	30	25
Other provision for dependants	12	10
Children's pension	27	22
Age reduction	42	34
Remarriage bar	9	7
Remarriage at or after retirement—no pension	10	8

(This table comes to more than 122 (100%) because more than one feature is present in some schemes.)

The conclusion must be that while the legal wife close in age to her husband can be catered for fairly well by many of these schemes, the common-law wife, the children of the late marriage, or the dependent relative of an unmarried member is still out in the cold, and it is for these that considerable work must be done.

The Occupational Pensions Board report on equal status went into considerable detail about the position of divorced and separated wives, and concluded that scheme rules should allow more flexibility in relation to allocating personal pensions or apportioning a survivor's pension between different beneficiaries and that new powers should be given to the courts to enable them to order that a survivor's pension should be paid in whole or in part to a divorced or separated spouse, or to order allocation from the member's personal pension. It remains to be seen whether in fact this will be incorporated into legislation.

INFLATION PROOFING OF PENSION ENTITLEMENTS

The contracting-out provisions include the alternative of using pension "excess" over the guaranteed minimum pension to pay for the cost of escalation of the GMP, but the use of this provision is a breach of the principle of pensions as deferred pay and should be strongly deprecated. It is important in the case of a contracted-out scheme for pension accrued before 1978 to be adequately funded for escalation, especially for those members who retire only a few years after 1978 with a small GMP for which the State provides inflation-proofing and perhaps a much larger pre-1978 pension for which the Company is solely responsible. The Inland Revenue will allow funding for no more than $8\frac{1}{2}\%$ escalation: one must hope that in future this level will be adequate to deal with inflation, though at times even trade unionists must have their doubts.

The GAD report found that some 35% of private sector schemes with pensioners covering 70% of members of such schemes provide some form of augmentation after retirement. Clearly augmentation is more likely to occur in the larger schemes. It is less frequent in manual schemes (the percentage of manual members covered being 55%) than in staff schemes for which the corresponding percentage is 75%. These figures show moderate growth since the 1967 inquiry. The pressure for increases may have been greater during 1967–71 than in earlier periods as the cost of living rose more rapidly. Yet some growth would in any case be expected with the passage of time because the need for increases would be more apparent as there came to be more persons who have been on pension for long enough to feel seriously affected by inflation.

In about three-quarters of private sector schemes the basis of augmentation was stated to be *ad hoc,* covering about two-thirds of members in such schemes. In some cases this might have been in addition to a contribution from surplus in the pension fund. In the remainder of cases the fund was given as the only source of finance. Where augmentation was automatic, however, reliance on the fund is rather greater, occurring in nearly one-half of such schemes covering one-third of their members. This doubtless indicates that advance provision is built up in the fund in many cases where augmentation is automatic.

The NAPF gave the percentage of schemes providing post-retirement increases shown in Table 16.

TABLE 16

	Staff schemes (%)	Works schemes (%)	Combined schemes (%)	All schemes (%)
Automatic increases	36	24	26	30
Non-automatic increases	45	37	56	47
No increases given	19	39	18	23

The table shows that 81% of staff schemes and 82% of combined schemes give post-retirement increases in pensions compared with only 61% of works schemes; staff schemes were most likely to provide increases on an automatic basis.

For those schemes which grant automatic escalation in pensions the most common level was 3% but under 4% with 58% of such schemes falling within this band. There were no significant differences between the classes of scheme in this sphere.

Larger schemes were found to be more likely to provide some increases in pensions, only 1 of the 97 staff and combined schemes with more than 5000 members having no such provision. The GMWU found that 76 schemes (62%) made no provision in their rules for the escalation of pensions in payment. (They may, however, have followed the custom of providing *ex-gratia* increases over the last few years.) Five further schemes pledged only a review to take account of the rise in the cost of living. The remainder guaranteed increases in percentage terms varying between 2½% and 5% provided the cost of living had risen by at least that much. Of these, 33 named the figure of 3% (but one stated that the increase was *ex gratia*). A small number of booklets made statements such as "the pension is paid at a higher rate from the outset instead of starting at a minimum rate with regular increases during retirement", a statement which now reads a little ironically in view of inflation.

The Pensions (Increase) Act 1971 of a Conservative Government provided for public servants' pensions to be increased in line with movements in the Retail Prices Index. Aided by trade union pressure the practice has been followed throughout the public sector.

At the outset subsequent rates of inflation were not envisaged, viz.:

1972	9.9%
1973	9.3%
1974	16.5%
1975	26.1%
1976	13.8%

Other evidence suggests that a number of large schemes or employers in the private sector, whilst not matching the above figures, have made substantial *ad hoc* increases to pensions in payment. Thus a position of envy has been created by the widening gap between the "haves" and "have nots", not to mention the constraints of pay code producing the anomaly of such pension increases exceeding pay awards.

Ensuring that pensions keep in line with the cost of living must be regarded as a worthwhile aspiration—not an object of jealousy. Known pressures for amending the Pensions (Increase) Act in the post-1977 budget came *other* than from the Labour Party, the TUC, and the unions.

TEMPORARY ABSENCE

There appear to be no statistics for the percentage of retirees with 40 years of service in one company, but Department of Employment figures in 1968 showed that only 37% of male manual workers, 43% of male non-manual had over 20 years of service, and that the figures were much lower for women. Some of these leavers would have taken a deferred pension, some a transfer value, but many would have had their contributions back and hopefully started again in a new scheme. In the future this will change due to the combination of the preservation requirements of the Social Security Act 1973 and/or the Castle scheme's contracting-out guaranteed minimum pension provisions.

The State scheme's earnings-related entitlements accumulating over the 20-year maturity period will cause a long-term re-distribution of income from the working to the non-working population. Almost certainly (in so far as any future government action can be certain) supplementary benefit level will be held at the level of the lower earnings limit in the new scheme, which will mean that the fall-back level for the retired population will be considerably lower than the average income of the employed population. Safeguarding the individual against any gap in his deferred pay is thus going to assume a new importance: gaps caused by such things as long-term sickness, lay-offs, and short-time working.

Too many occupational schemes deal inadequately with any form of temporary absence. As many as 43% of the GMWU sample did not mention it; others merely stated that contributions would be suspended and the ultimate pension reduced. If we are to be serious about providing lifetime earnings-related pensions for all we must be sure that our schemes cater for industries with a high risk of sickness, accident, or recession as well as for the "average" industry.

The GMWU survey (1976) for the Occupational Pensions Board found the following position:

- No provision specified, 43%.
- Life assurance continues, 19%.
- Membership continues, provision for arrears to be made up, 22.5%.
- Company pays or contributions come from disability payments, 5.5%.
- At discretion, 8.5%.
- Membership continues, arrears not payable, 12%.

This adds up to more than 100% because of overlapping features in some cases. In addition there were a few schemes where there was clearly some provision, but the information given was vague, e.g. "you will remain a member while away sick". It is of the greatest importance that the relevant provisions are spelt out clearly, as the onset of illness causes sufficient anxiety about the future without needless additional concern.

Some of the employments where no provision was specific in the pension scheme will have adequate sick-pay schemes but others will not. Even those with provision sometimes have it extending over a too limiting term—in one case only 6 weeks' absence, in another case only 4, after which even the death-in-service cover terminated.

There is obvious need for early concentration on two fronts: firstly, adequate coverage of temporary absence in the pension scheme; and, secondly, the introduction of more reasonable sick-pay schemes for manual workers.

Figures from the General Household survey 1972 show that whereas 99.6% of professional employees are covered by sick-pay arrangements run by their employers, less than 55% of manual workers are. Industrial Relations Review and Report surveyed the field in 1973 and commented: "In general, the harder physical working conditions are, the less valuable sick pay provisions are likely to be. This is shown most clearly in the advantages enjoyed by white collar workers over manual workers. Thus provisions are most generous in the financial sector and in capital intensive industries, least generous in metals, engineering and construction."

The exemptions of improvements in sick-pay schemes from the pay-policy guidelines for 1976/7 will undoubtedly have given impetus to the inauguration and improvement of such schemes although it will be some time before confirming figures become available.

CONCLUSIONS

All the issues contained in this chapter are target levels of benefit which can be achieved either by contracting out or by full participation in the State scheme and riding an efficient occupational scheme on top.

The decision on contracting in or out is not a clear-cut one. It is marginal, depending upon the circumstances of each individual scheme and the industry concerned with the balance of advantages and disadvantages to be weighed in each case (see Chapter 2).

In this discussion of aspirations it would have been wrong to lay down a blueprint or a model scheme that we *must* have at any price. That would be a mistake and out of step with the flexible approach which one should endeavour to maintain. I have tried to show the level of benefits one should seek—a fairly high level but not an impossibly high one.

The planned approach to pension schemes being central to collective bargaining must be to determine:

(1)   The "target" of retirement income to be provided by the State and the occupational scheme.

(2)   The "mix" of the benefits, i.e. the proportion from the State and the occupational scheme determined by the contract-in or contract-out decision.

(3)   The apportionment of the cost between the employer and the employees, which in itself determines the proportion of the negotiated cost of labour that is applied to deferred pay.

No easy task against a background of:

- fiscal constraints
- pay-code constraints or the aftermath
- social insurance contributions having to provide acceptable levels of benefits for the unacceptable level of unemployed
- unpredictable inflation

but not impossible provided that it is generally understood that, unlike wage bargaining timed to last for a 12-month period at the most, the pension scheme has to attempt to balance the needs of those whose efforts in the past have made the scheme possible with the aspirations of younger employees to whom retirement is 40 years or more away.

CHAPTER 7

Negotiated Schemes—Specific Cases

It has been suggested that it would be appropriate to illustrate typical cases of negotiation over recent times between management and unions on pensions. In the main these negotiations were an entirely new departure, particularly for the manual unions, and the two cases that I have selected are from a total numbering hundreds with personal involvement.

Both cases, however, illustrate important aspects of negotiation, involving at times considerable differences of opinion. They are intended to illustrate that despite differences, *without industrial strife,* negotiations have been brought to a successful conclusion and schemes introduced. Equally important is that in each case the unions have given the strongest possible recommendation for their members to take the opportunity of joining the scheme that has been subject to the negotiations.

Should any particular event in the chain of negotiations in respect of any of these case studies be quoted in isolation and out of context, it can but be harmful to the hard-won amicable relationships which now exist.

PILKINGTON

This is a company with about 10,000 hourly paid workers with whom the GMWU has a considerable involvement. A strike within Pilkington in 1970 was a traumatic experience for Company and union officials alike. A long-standing harmonious relationship had apparently taken insufficient notice of the "grass roots" feelings— an experience which resulted in a more democratic approach to all subsequent negotiations.

The manual workers at Pilkington had been brought into a pension scheme as early as 1925. By 1973 it was based on a two-tier money purchase system (there have been member trustees since its inception), the first tier being a 10p a week compulsory scheme, the second a voluntary scheme with contributions ranging up to 90p a week. Only 20% of employees failed to make an additional voluntary contribution over the minimum rate. Death in service cover was £750. There was, in addition, a separate scheme at Triplex Limited which had been taken over by the Company in the recent past when these particular negotiations commenced in mid-1973.

HISTORY OF NEGOTIATIONS

In May 1973 the Company issued a Green Paper entitled *Consultation Document on Pensions Policy.* This was based on the assumption that the Sir Keith Joseph State Reserve Scheme would come into effect in April 1975. The Company proposed a single "all embracing scheme" for manual and staff employees, but on a two-tier basis, providing 100ths and 50ths integrated at one and a half times the State basic pensions. In June 1973 a preliminary meeting was held which discussed both the disposal of the surplus on the current Workmen's Pension Fund and the Company's latest proposals.

The unions took the view that they were acceptable in principle but needed alteration in terms of the State pension disregard and the two-tier structure. Despite original pressure from the Company for agreement by October 1973 the discussion hung fire until Spring 1974, when a written response was made by the GMWU seeking a number of changes. The first meeting on this union's proposals was not held until the original Green Paper's proposals had been overtaken by events with the abandonment of the State Reserve Scheme in May 1974 by the incoming Labour Government.

In August 1974 the Company promised to produce a further paper for the unions to consider but instead, in October of that year, the Company advised that it had decided to postpone, at least until 1976, the implementation of pensions policy. It had been announced that the Government did not intend to implement the Sir Keith Joseph Reserve Scheme upon which the Company's proposal had been based. A pointed discussion therefore took place later that year at a meeting previously called to deal with industrial relations matters at which the unions said they found it difficult to understand why the Company had decided on this course of action without prior consultation; as a result it was agreed that a joint working party of Company and union representatives, primarily consisting of specialists, should be set up. It would need to report back to the GMWU's negotiating committee, since that body would have to answer questions from the membership.

The working party's terms of reference were: "to establish what improvements to existing death-in-service arrangements could be introduced in April 1975 and report on long-term pensions implications."

In December 1974 the first meeting of this working party was held. Contrary to the normal negotiating practice within Pilkington this covered both staff and non-staff representatives. At this meeting the Company made a single proposal that the death-in-service benefit should be increased from £750 to £1500. It was stated that the Company believed that there should be a sensible relationship between death benefits and pension rights and they were not in favour of dealing with either of these elements in isolation. The Company certainly did not feel that it was right to substitute a multiple of annual pay for the £750 because in the case of hourly paid personnel any such multiple would be disproportionately high in both cost and benefit. It would also lead to anomalies in that it would produce a situation whereby the widow of a man dying in service shortly before retirement would receive a large lump sum but the widow of a man dying shortly after retirement would receive nothing.

The unions responded that they found the Company's proposal totally unacceptable bearing in mind that the average gross pay was £2600 per annum. The existing death benefit was related to the Boyd-Carpenter contracted-out scheme which would in any case cease on 5 April 1975. The unions made a counter-proposal of a group life scheme of twice PAYE earnings plus a group accident scheme also with a benefit twice PAYE earnings.

Subject to reaching agreement on this current proposal the unions undertook to publicise the value of joining the voluntary pension scheme as an interim measure, i.e. until the 1978 contracting-out decision had been resolved.

It was agreed that the matter should be referred to the Company's Board in January, and that the next meeting of the working party would be arranged as early as possible in February 1975. However, in February the Company merely reiterated by letter their offer to increase life cover to £1500. A deadlock arose with the unions repeating *their* view that "the Company's offer of a lump sum death in service benefit of £1500 is quite unacceptable; not only is it out of step with industry in general, but it is far removed from the aims and desires of the Unions and our membership—in particular that within Pilkington hourly paid employees—that they should be provided with the same level of benefits as members in the staff scheme."

In March the Company wrote to the unions:

"The existing life cover of £750 for your members has, up to now, been provided by the Pilkington (Contracted out) Pension Scheme. This scheme will terminate on 5th April, next. It is our intention nevertheless to continue the life cover of £750 but we need to hear from you before the 24th of this month as to whether you accept our offer to raise this from £750 to £1,500 as an interim improvement. The most convenient method available to us after 5th April would be through the existing Pilkington Workmen's Pension Fund so that we hope that for the time being we can reach universal agreement to make this improvement for all non-staff employees with effect from that date."

Substantial further progress was, however, within grasp, as the

Company gave the first indication of a willingness to consider further interim improvements "designed so that they can operate either on top of the State proposals or as a suitable method of contracting out if this proves to be the more appropriate course of action". They added that "in particular we intend to put a proposal to you for a scheme to pay a lump sum at normal retirement age...".

The union, in what was now a very difficult situation, replied to the effect:

(1) The current year's wages submission which has yet to be formulated must now take account of the fact that you are maintaining the position of refusing to negotiate on pensions.

(2) It was not made clear by the Company's representatives at the meeting of the pensions working party held on 12 December 1974 that the proposed improvement in the death-in-service benefit from £750 to £1500 from April 1975 was offered on a "take-it-or-leave-it" basis.

(3) Notwithstanding our strongly held views that even as an interim measure a death-in-service benefit of £1500 is regarded as inadequate by both the union and its membership within your Company, we do not wish to impede the introduction of this level of benefit from the 6 April 1975.

(4) Your letter under acknowledgement gives the first advice of your intention to put forward a proposal, for implementation from January 1976, for a scheme for the hourly paid, to pay a lump sum at normal retirement age with consideration to be given to improve further the £1500 death-in-service benefit. This information would have been of considerable assistance had it been made available for consideration in conjunction with your letter of the 14 February 1975.

(5) In accepting the interim situation may we therefore ask that you confirm:

(a) that our members be given a full explanation of the death-in-service benefit being increased to only a figure of £1500 from the 6 April 1975 (as previously advised

their anticipations will be for a benefit of not less than
that enjoyed by your staff employees);

(b) that the proposals to be forthcoming for implementation from 1 January 1976 will be subject to negotiation
with the unions which will then lead us properly into the
position of considering jointly the implications of contracting in or out of the new State scheme.

The Company therefore went ahead with the death-in-service
benefit improvement and called another meeting in May 1975. The
Group Pensions Adviser stated in advance:

"At this meeting I will present an outline of the Company's
proposals for a further interim improvement in non-staff pension
arrangements along the lines of providing a lump sum on retirement. I will seek to demonstrate how the Company sees this
proposal as keeping options open for further development in terms
of integration with our staff employees pension arrangements. I
hope that this will lead to a series of meetings of the Joint Working
Party enabling us to develop satisfactory consultation with you
upon future pension arrangements against the background of the
Social Security Pensions Bill."

The meeting virtually developed into a dialogue between each
side's pensions advisers with other unions supporting the GMWU's
lead.

As at a previous meeting there was discussion once more as to the
precise status of the working party. The Company stated that they
wished to find a satisfactory method of consultation with the unions
on pensions and saw the working party principally as a fact-finding
body. They accepted that they would be expected to take the initiative
in putting the proposals to the union representatives on the working
party. Some of these would be firm proposals which they would be
prepared to implement if an acceptable basis could be agreed with the
unions. It was agreed that the members of the working party would
require freedom to examine various possibilities and their implications without committing their respective sides to obligations which

would require ratification by either the Company or the union membership.

On the Company's firm proposals their representatives commenced by outlining their philosophy. The Company was not prepared to accept any open-ended financial commitment in the pensions area. They were not prepared to establish pension proposals on a balance of cost basis in which the Company would guarantee the benefits to emerge or to enter into any commitment to augment pensions so as to match inflation. Security of employment is more important than creating a high standard of pension provision; the national officers of the unions had been kept informed by the Company of the state of trade and were aware of the potential limitations on improvements to pension. It was still the Company's aim to create one pension scheme for all employees if possible. Included in the Company's philosophy was what it described as "a total pay concept"; namely, that the cost of providing a given range of pension benefits is part of the cost of employment. For this reason, pensions must become negotiable, but they cannot be dealt with in isolation and without reference to their cost implications in terms of wage claims and investment needs which provide continuity of employment. Particular care is needed because of the long-term implications of pension costs which are capable of depriving negotiators of options in the future. For this reason, "balance of cost" is inappropriate and subvention payments or anything else which is fundamentally in the gift of the Company must be excluded as possibilities. If pensions are to be negotiated, the forward financial commitments must be precise and must be recognised by both sides.

The meeting then proceeded to consider the Company's proposal for a lump-sum scheme at retirement based on 3/80ths of the employee's final salary for each complete year of service subsequent to 1 January 1976 with a maximum payment of 120/80ths for 40 years of service. The proposal included group life cover at one and a half times pay for members against the risk of death in service. This was intended to be made available to all United Kingdom employees in the Pilkington Group who are not eligible for membership of the Pilkington Superannuation Scheme.

It was clear that the Company did not intend to guarantee that the lump-sum retirement benefit would emerge at the level proposed. What was proposed was a contribution-based scheme in which the retirement benefit ultimately to emerge would depend entirely upon what the contributions produced and in effect upon the accuracy of the underlying actuarial assumptions. Necessarily, therefore, much of the discussion at this and future meetings centred around this assumption and the precise costing of different items. A serious drawback from the unions' standpoint was the absence of a proposal for a lump sum of one and a half times pay in the event of permanent total disablement.

The unions firmly expressed the view that a scheme of this sort— costed by the Company at 2.25% of pay roll—should be non-contributory for the members. The Company reserved its position on this item which was left over to subsequent meetings.

Following this meeting, feedback to the unions from local level made it clear that there was some disquiet as to the possible remoteness of the working party, not only from the ordinary negotiating machinery but also from the member trustees. For this reason before the next working party meeting a discussion was held between the union's pensions specialist and the members' representatives on the committee of the Workmen's Pension Fund. This covered three points:

(1)   the members' representatives' opinion of the proposed 3/80ths package;

(2)   whether the package should be considered as part of the total wage claim;

(3)   their opinion of the Company's proposals for simplification of existing pension arrangements.

Of these points item (2) was probably the most fundamental and it was an issue where the separate role of the working party was most tricky. The general view was that pensions should not be part of a wage deal, but that if they needed to be considered as such then it was a matter for the negotiating committee and *not* the working party. It might in fact have to go to a ballot of members. In reality the matter was not pressed by the Company in this acute form, but the Company insisted that its "total pay concept" was the only valid basis for negotiation of pension rights.

Generally the members' representatives were in favour of the Company's proposals although they were concerned to achieve an improved early retirement benefit. On this basis negotiations were able to continue over two subsequent meetings until a final package emerged including the disablement benefit previously proposed by the unions. The final package on a non-contributory basis included the following benefits:

(a) lump sum on retirement up to one and a half times final pay for 40 years of service;

(b) lump-sum payment on early retirement on grounds of ill health or any other grounds when over 55 years of age;

(c) insurance against death or permanent total disability whilst in service—one and a half times the previous tax year's PAYE earnings;

(d) the scheme to be administered by a 50/50 committee of management and unions.

The scheme was introduced in February 1976 with the Company's contribution fixed at 3% of pay roll. Not unexpectedly the discussions on the new scheme led on to consultation upon contracting in or out. The scheme as at present constituted would be suitable either for contracting in and "riding on top" or as a basis on which to build a full contracted-out pension scheme. The scheme has been used as a model for the "minimum" type of "ride-on-top" scheme complementary to full participation in the State scheme which the union was willing to negotiate elsewhere in industry.

After detailed consultation with the Company providing all relevant information to the unions, and the latter having received all the members' representatives' views at a meeting arranged for the purpose, it has been decided to contract-in in April 1978. The decision is to be related to a commitment to continue negotiations on the overall pension provision as financial conditions permit.

It is encouraging to note that the member trustees are now much more fully involved in administration of the scheme than they were previously—especially on the investment side. In fact the unions and trustees have been in some disagreement upon the White Paper on membership participation—not on the principle but on the details—and this is really a healthy sign of a much livelier member presence than existed before pensions in Pilkington became fully negotiable.

COMMENT

The history of these negotiations is a satisfactory one in that a successful outcome was reached and a close working relationship established. The early negotiations bore the hallmarks of a Company not used to negotiating on pensions, but subsequent advances have indicated that the union's role is now fully accepted.

The pattern of negotiations with pension specialists conducting virtually all the discussions highlights the need for a greater attention being paid by both management and unions to concentrating on pensions training at all levels. Industrial relations staff, on the one hand, and stewards and full-time union officials, on the other, must get themselves fully acquainted with all aspects of pensions. Pensions negotiations cannot be handled in the same way as wage negotiations. The outcome is not a 12-month agreement but a range of benefits that must be planned, costed, and supported until the youngest member of the workforce qualifies for pension.

GKN PENSIONS AND THE UNIONS REPRESENTING THE MANUAL WORKERS

This case study is of a very large engineering group based mainly in the Midlands, the mannual workers' force being some 66,000 in total, covering some 150 plants and subsidiary companies. There were representatives from 15 national unions at the first meeting in 1974.

As with others mentioned in this book, the Group had a history of mergers and take-overs, additionally complicated in their case by nationalisation of their steel interests. Towards the close of 1973 an announcement was issued to works employees of improvements to the manual workers' pension and death benefit arrangements to be implemented from 1 July 1974. These improvements had not been negotiated with the unions at any level. The Group proposed to put in train an extensive consultation programme before July. The announcement said they would early in 1974 arrange consultation on the improved arrangements with employees' representatives at individual companies when the new plan would be discussed and there would be opportunities for questions to be raised and comments made. Following this they would arrange with companies times and dates of meetings when the plan would be further explained to groups of employees. As there were over 150 company locations in the GKN Group the programme of meetings would take at least 2 months to complete. They would then complete the arrangements in respect of the new plan (including contracting out of the optional part of the State graduated pension scheme), obtain Inland Revenue approval, and also the approval of the Occupational Pensions Board.

As the Group's consultation programme got under way inquiries from members regarding the scheme flooded into the various union headquarters. Following informal discussions between the unions in April 1974 it was agreed that the AUEW should take the initiative in calling for a meeting with the Group of all the unions concerned. This was one of the first company-wide meetings arranged and it was something of a step in the dark for the unions.

Between the calling of the meeting and the meeting itself, Mrs. Castle's announcement of the abandonment of the State Reserve Scheme was made. In the light of this change of circumstances, GKN issued to all employees a leaflet explaining this and giving everyone the chance to reappraise the situation before committing themselves to joining. A booklet was also issued to all participating employees explaining in detail all the arrangements as they applied at the time. One of the paragraphs read: "you start to contribute on the 1st July on which day you join the plan and continue until normal retiring date or until you leave service if earlier."

The outcome of the first meeting between the unions and the GKN management can best be recalled by quoting from the announcement sent out afterwards by the unions to their members: "While appreciating the uniqueness of the occasion and recognising that the Company had already carried through an extensive Communication Exercise at most of their Plants, where they explained the basis of their Pension Plan, nevertheless, the Unions required this meeting in order to improve, where possible, and to discuss in general the views of their membership on the total Scheme and seek to arrive at an agreed understanding." Since the publication in December 1973 of the Company's plan, many employees had indicated their intention to join; also on 7 May 1974 the Government had announced a significant change in the 1973 Social Security Act which directly affected the situation in so far as the proposed State Reserve Scheme had been rescinded and occupational pension schemes were not as a consequence required to meet certain standards for exemption.

HISTORY OF NEGOTIATIONS

The unions identified the features of the pension plan on which they sought clarity and, where possible, improvement. They also indicated additional matters including right of representation, back service to count, and detailed information to ensure that the plan provided for the membership value for money.

In the course of the detailed discussion the Company recognised the various issues and new features which the unions had drawn to their attention. There were a number of basic matters which they undertook to give sympathetic attention to, including a form of representation, the problems confronting older employees, possible widow's pension when death in service occurs, and the clarification of additional features.

Certain information they stated would not be available until they knew the numbers that would enter the scheme by the prescribed date of 1 July 1974. The unions then questioned the works notice which set an expiry date of 26 May 1974, and the Company agreed that entry into the new plan was open until 30 June 1974.

Having regard to the progress of these discussions, coupled with the undertakings given by the Company, the unions were of the opinion that in all the prevailing circumstances the membership should be advised to join the scheme "subject to their own personal considerations and commitments".

The scheme is on an integrated 1/60ths formula with a death-in-service lump sum and death-in-retirement widow's pension. The immediate result to emerge at the first meeting was that additional pension under the old flat-rate scheme was provided for those who were within 10 years of retirement. The increase was generous in percentage terms, from £5.20 per year of service to £8 for men, and from £3.90 to £6 for women, although the pension provided was still modest. Part-timers were now allowed to join the new scheme, and the pensionable earnings formula was adjusted.

The negotiations were amicable and were off to a good start. At the next meeting in July 1974 this amicable feeling remained. A detailed discussion took place on member representation. Again, both unions and management were breaking new ground and had no previous model from which to work. The following principles were established during the discussion: that member trustees would be appointed from among members of the works pension plan with the number and method of selection to be determined, and that the trade unions would be given an opportunity to consider the plan rules in draft form and to comment. In order to avoid the creation of cumbersome consultative machinery at works level, pension consultative committees would be established at subgroup level—one for each of the fourteen subgroups, with possibly a fifteenth committee to serve future fund members employed by recently acquired companies.

It was appreciated that the selection of plan member representatives could present a complex problem because of the structure of the Company and the distribution of trade union membership. Therefore the meeting appointed a nine-member working party who were instructed to identify and consider the problem of subgroup representations and to report to the meeting.

It was agreed that the meeting between the Company and the national officers of the trade unions should be reconvened at least once per year to examine pensions policy and to review the progress of the GKN works pension plan.

The above principles have in fact been used as guidelines for many other situations since. One problem that arose in the subsequent discussions was that the initial costing of the plan had been based on the proportions of members known to have joined other big schemes. The initial estimated cost had been £2.2 million. With the greater interest being taken in the plan resulting in higher membership, and with the changes that had been made, it was now known that the real initial cost would be £4 million. In these circumstances any further concessions, no matter how desirable, would have to lie on the table until the situation was clearer. It was proposed that both sides should state which of the residual matters they regarded as the most outstanding, not necessarily in a strict order of priority; both sides could then keep these particular items constantly under review.

A list of these residual matters was then drawn up with the unions taking the view that the redefinition of final pensionable earnings (from the best 5 years in the last 10 to the best 3) could be conceded immediately. The Company were surprised at this choice, but agreed to consider it.

In fact this amendment was subsequently included with others agreed at national meetings held on 29th January 1975 and 20 May 1975. Other improvements agreed at these meetings for implementation on 1 July 1975 (or earlier) included:

(1) Early retirement through serious ill health. The pension calculation was amended to include one-half of uncompleted service between the date of retirement and normal retirement date.

(2) Dependant's pension on death of a female pensioner is now granted where genuine financial dependency can be established.

(3) Post-retirement widow's pension was increased from one-third to one-half of the member's gross pension with effect from 1 July 1974.

A continuing review of other priority items was undertaken and has continued in subsequent meetings between GKN management and the national officials of major unions represented in the Group. It is to be expected that as soon as Pay Code restrictions permit there will be an agreed increase in additional past-service pensions for the older employees.

THE CONSULTATIVE STRUCTURE

At the meeting of the working party set up on 14 August 1974 the issue of consultative structures was taken in detail. The complexity of the Group meant that a high degree of flexibility was needed. It was fully accepted that the composition of any subgroup consultative committee would have to have regard for several different factors, including strength of individual union representation, number and sizes of companies making up the subgroup, geographical spread, etc. It was acknowledged that the various factors were likely to carry significantly differing weighting in the different subgroups. An example of a possible structure for the Fastener subgroups consultative committee was quoted for illustrative purposes, viz. 11,000 potential pension scheme members in 19 companies located in the West Midlands, Leicester, Cardiff, Glasgow, etc., involving 5 major unions, and justifying a consultative committee composed of 13 member representatives plus 3 from management.

It was agreed that the terms of reference of all consultative committees might include:

(a) the provision of a reference point for the interpretation of the rules of the scheme;

(b) the provision of a forum for reference of individual cases of special difficulties and complexity;

(c) the responsibility for acting as a sounding board and channel for recommendations on improvements to the scheme;

(d)   the responsibility for furthering a greater understanding and awareness of pension matters.

At the next meeting the Company produced a draft procedure. It was noticeable how even at this stage the Company appeared deeply concerned about the repercussions at local level if they were seen as "imposing" anything from the centre. The draft said:

"This Pension Plan is essentially a personal matter and as such the consultative procedures set out below seek to take care of the individual and in so doing give expression to the interests of all.

"It is suggested that the consultative advisory procedure be based upon two levels:

(a)   Plant Consultative Committee

(b)   Sub Group Consultative Committee

both of which would have ready access to the Group Pensions Office. For consideration and ultimate implementation (if approved by the parties concerned) are certain suggestions as to how this two tier level might operate in practice.

"Plant Consultative Committee
"(i)   it would be the responsibility of the Unions and the Management of the plant concerned to agree on the appropriate members and numbers of this Committee but it is suggested that there be equal representation from both management and membership and that, in addition, the Company should nominate the Chairman of such committee;

(ii)   the members of the Committee progressively, over a period of time (educational facilities being provided by the Company) build up a degree of detailed knowledge of the practical side of the Works Pension Plan and thus play an ever increasing part in an advisory role within the plant;

(iii)   typical terms of reference should include the following—

(a)   to agree the basis used for arriving at the earnings figure to be used for life assurance benefits for new engagements, in the period prior to entry to the Plan;

(b) to agree upon the consultative procedure to be followed when, annually, the statement is made to each contributor of the earnings to be used for contributions, pension and life assurance benefit in the following Pension Year;

(c) to agree upon the administrative procedure to be followed in giving an annual statement to the member of contributions made to date and prospective pension;

(d) an understanding of the method by which arrears in contributions are collected;

(e) agree a recommendation to the trustees on the disposal of any life assurance benefits where there is a question as to the appropriate dependant;

(f) consider the advisability of an advisory service for the dependants of deceased persons;

(g) agree upon advisory service for members prior to their retirement;

(h) have ready access to Sub group/Group where a point of detail of principle has arisen which in their view requires an immediate ruling;

(i) the proceedings to be recorded and the frequency of meetings of this Plant Consultative Committee left entirely to the discretion of the Committee itself.

"Sub Group Consultative Committee

"(i) It is suggested that this committee should meet annually under the Chairmanship of the Sub Group Administrative Director. Its membership should consist of management and member representatives from each of the Plant Consultative committees within the sub group. It is further proposed that the G.K.N. Group Pensions Officer should, *ex officio*, be a member of this committee.

(ii) This committee would have broad terms of reference but in general should cover the following subject matters:

(a) receive from the sub group administrative director a

report of the operation of the Works Pension Plan during the preceding twelve months, laying particular
emphasis on problems that have arisen and the manner
and form in which the problems were resolved;

(b) consider any points of principle raised by any member of
this committee and see that the resultant discussion on
such points of principle either reached resolution
through the presence of the G.K.N. Pensions Officer or,
if not, then the issue should be carried forward for
consideration in due course at the National meeting.''

The union responded to these proposals with detailed comments
that it was necessary that they should have the suggested terms of
reference for the National Committee in order that they determine
proper liaison with the other committees. The chairman of the Plant
Consultative Committee should be elected by members of the
committee not nominated by the Company. Similarly, provisions
should be made for the members to elect a secretary of that committee. Members of the committee should hold office for an agreed
period of time, ideally not less than 3 years but not more than 5 years.
Mention is made of educational provisions being made by the
Company; it was imperative for the unions to be involved to ensure
that the education provided was in pursuit of TUC policy on these
matters. The terms of reference should include recommendation to
the trustees in respect of exercising their other discretionary powers
in addition to any life assurance benefits where there is a question as
to the appropriate dependant. The Subgroup Consultative Committee should be responsible for electing their own chairman with the
subgroup administrative director being an *ex officio* member of the
committee as was proposed for the group pensions officer. The
committee should receive from the subgroup administrative director
a report of the policy and the performance of the fund along with
copies of the annual accounts for consideration.

Most of these items were agreed by the Company at subsequent
meetings.

The proposals were ratified by the rest of the unions involved in

January 1975 at which, after considerable debate, it was agreed that, subject to endorsement of the proposals by each of the unions, the working party would meet again to agree a joint working document which would be distributed to explain the implementation of the advisory/consultative procedures.

The Company confirmed their acceptance of member participation in the trusteeship. It was agreed to refer this subject to the joint working party already established for discussion on numbers, methods of appointment, and member trustees' responsibilities.

When the working party met in March it was able to deal in considerable detail with the working document. They found some difficulty, however, because by no means all the unions had as yet endorsed the progress so far achieved and the general principles of the consultative procedure. It was unfortunately not uncommon for unions even when they had taken an active part in discussions to be extremely slow in providing any written documentation needed.

Left outstanding at this meeting was the detailed question of the trustees. The Company were asked to elaborate upon their proposals under various headings. One further meeting resolved this issue and the working party was then able to take the question back to the full body for endorsement in May 1975; here it was agreed that the appointment of member trustees was not immediately pressing but the appointments should be made before the end of the year.

Plant committees should *nominate* candidates for appointment and subgroup/committees should have the right to scrutinise the nominations and submit those they considered suitable to the national meeting. The trade union side of the national meeting would compile a list of 5 to 7 nominees and then reach agreement on the composition of the list with the Company representatives. The trade union members suggested that the agreed list should be submitted to the fund members for endorsement, but the Company representatives expressed reservations about the practicality of the proposal.

The discussion turned to the problem of striking the right balance in the constitution of the subgroup committees. It was agreed that, with the possible exception of the Brymbo Steel Works Limited and Firth Cleveland Limited, subgroup committees should consist of one representative per plant committee. The difficulties of setting up a structure of this sort was well illustrated by these two.

Brymbo Steel Works Limited consisted of 1800 employees in one plant and constituted a subgroup *per se*; the plant committee would therefore be sufficient for consultative purposes.

Firth Cleveland Limited. This subgroup consisted of no less than 40 plants, some employing very few employees, the overall total being 3600. It was agreed that the pensions consultative arrangements for this subgroup may have to be re-examined in consultation with the subgroup management.

It was agreed that the formation of plant committees to be given priority in the interests of directly involving members in pensions consultation procedures as early as possible and that the constitution of subgroup committees was less urgent and required further consideration. It was a matter for trade union members to face up to their responsibility and to seek nomination as members of consultative committees and as trustees.

Selection of trustees did not therefore take place until June 1976 when all the consultative committees had been established and started functioning. The Company arranged and paid for all the member trustees to attend a pensions course run by one of the unions involved. The scheme is now set in a regular and smooth-running pattern. There is provision in the procedure agreement for annual meetings of national officials; all administrative and personal matters are being channelled within the consultative structure.

LOCAL DIFFICULTIES

Mention should also be made of the various meetings and discussions held at different plants around the country. These meetings were separate from the Company's own consultative ones and were held primarily in response to requests from union members. In part they were report-back meetings and partly an educational exercise in which the unions' officials had to convince their members as to the value of the GKN plan.

Other contentious issues included a demand for a special formula to provide "value for money" pensions for those members who were compelled to move down from a well-paid but physically demanding job to a lower-paid job at an age prior to the final salary formula becoming operative. A special formula was agreed by the Inland Revenue Authorities to meet these particular circumstances.

Despite the excellent range of benefits in the scheme, frequent demands for withdrawal were received from members whose pay packets had reduced because of unavailability of overtime, seeking to reduce their total deductions. The unions repeatedly had to advise members that contributions could not be refunded whilst remaining in the employment of GKN.

However, the negotiating role of the manual unions with GKN is now well established and based on a harmonious working relationship.

COMMENT

Throughout the meetings with GKN and British Leyland (see page 99) John Foster, National Officer of the AUEW, chaired the trade union side with considerable knowledge and ability, the successful conclusion giving proof that an experienced industrial negotiator, with studied application, can add pensions to his range of skills.

GENERAL CONCLUSION

I appreciate that these two case studies are of large work forces—multi-union, multi-plant, and engaged in manual or craft occupations. The principles established and the lessons that have been learnt can equally be related to much smaller companies with employees numbered in hundreds rather than thousands.

It has been proved that the trade unions representing hourly paid workers have contributed to the growth in pension schemes, to be measured in the additional number of potential beneficiaries and prospective pensioners, particularly during the past 4 years. Despite the change in the shape of the State scheme, and despite the restricting elements of the pay policy, new pension schemes have been negotiated, inaugurated, or amended.

Evidence abounds that a scheme which is negotiated and thereby recommended by the unions to their membership is more readily appreciated subject to a well-organised communications exercise, including clear explanatory booklets.

Negotiated membership participation in the running of such schemes is but a natural consequence, extending to education and training, thus removing barriers and with them suspicions that can surround even good schemes.

CHAPTER 8

The Way Ahead

There is little doubt that pensions have moved firmly into a new arena and will remain so—perhaps for the rest of the twentieth century—at least until the maturity of the Castle Plan should that ever be advanced from the present 1998 date.

An all-party agreement on the main provisions of the Social Security Pensions Act 1975 is understood to exist. The Conservative Party have stated, both in and outside the House of Commons, that they will not scrap the new State scheme and the Liberal Party has accepted the scheme's main provisions.

The trade unions are supporting the Government by discouraging bare-bones occupational schemes, i.e. those with benefits at the minimum level for the purpose of contracting out. The unions are, however, endorsing decisions by employers with good schemes to contract out.

These attitudes can be taken as an acceptance of a mixed economy being desirable, with a realisation that the present generation of workers would eventually call a halt should increases in Social Insurance contributions to the State reduce take-home pay to below subsistence level—an obvious happening, should the State scheme be made to provide a vastly improved range of benefits, particularly at an earlier age for men.

Whilst the State scheme remains on a pay-as-you-go basis, complementary funded occupational schemes are essential. Investments of pension funds properly and fully utilised—not just used to play the "money game"—should provide factories, shops, offices, private dwellings, and jobs, producing the ability (given the willingness) to pay existing pensioners at rates in keeping with the wage-earners' aspirations.

The key to the future lies in the success or otherwise of the attack on inflation. If one takes the view that the rate of inflation experienced over the past 3 years will continue in the long term, that the rate of return on investments will not exceed the rate of justifiable increases in earnings—then contracting out is ill-advised because funded occupational schemes could not survive.

Such a view, an extremely pessimistic one, has drastic implications for the nation's economy as a whole, not just the funding of pension schemes. To write this book, let alone read it, one must take the view that the rate of inflation will be reduced to a level below that of the rate of return on investments.

Once that objective has been achieved with certainty, then the trade unions will be concentrating on the two areas within pensions where a committed consensus exists, viz.:

(1) Pensions are deferred pay and therefore should be central to collective bargaining and fully negotiated. Contracted-out schemes at or approaching minimum level of benefits will be used as a launching pad to negotiate a range of benefits comparable with those provided in the public sector.

(2) Members of schemes should have the right to participate at least on a 50/50 basis in the management of their deferred pay. Should anticipated legislation be delayed or not materialise in order to enforce the entitlement on reluctant employers, sufficient advances have been made with leading national employers in negotiating effective membership participation schemes *without any industrial strife* to ensure that the practice must gain momentum.

Negotiated pension schemes and negotiated membership participation structures could and should provide a "bridge" between capitalism and organised labour—a bridge, with proper construction, to produce the greatest industrial advance this century.

It is long overdue. The gap between the implementation of Beveridge 1948 and the Castle Plan in 1978 is a credit to no one. The hotch-potch growth of occupational pensions in that same period has produced the anomalies of the four-class retirement society:

First: the public sector schemes providing pensions increased in line with increases in the Retail Prices Index. I in no way support the politics of envy that is repeatedly aroused, but it must be appreciated that these model schemes are provided at the expense of the taxpayer, the rate payer, and the consumers of monopoly industries.

Second: private sector schemes with pensions increased as of right at varying rates of up to 5% per annum compound or on an *ex gratia* basis by trustees and/or management who have made serious attempts to alleviate the plight of pensioners as prices have soared.

Third: private sector schemes where employers provide pensions at minimum cost and do not increase pensions in payment.

Fourth: those in retirement with no occupational pensions at all, remembering that at the time of the last survey of the Government Actuary in 1971 10 million workers had no entitlement to occupational pensions, 2 million of them having to rely on supplementary benefits to exist. A further three-quarters of a million or more pensioners do not claim their supplementary benefit, either for reasons of pride or ignorance of their entitlements.

There are obvious gaps to be closed in the differing scales of retirement benefits and I in no way support any levelling down of entitlements. Pensions will remain a problem of social conscience until these anomalies are tackled with a greater degree of urgency than at present exists, yet pensions demands must be moderated in order that jobs should not be put at risk.

There are yawning chasms in the understanding, communicating, educating, and training of the countless numbers who are involved in pensions and all who are entitled to these benefits.

I hope this book is a small contribution towards a daunting task.

Percentage in Each Industry of Full-time Employees covered by Occupational Pension Schemes, April 1970

	Manual		Non-manual	
INDUSTRY	Men (%)	Women (%)	Men (%)	Women (%)
Manufacturing industries				
Food, drink, and tobacco	59.7	21.6	76.9	32.7
Coal and petroleum products	69.2	38.0	85.4	45.1
Chemicals and allied industries	75.1	34.7	83.6	45.9
Metal manufacture	61.5	28.3	79.6	42.7
Mechanical engineering	46.7	20.4	69.8	26.9
Instrument engineering	44.6	18.7	62.0	30.3
Electrical engineering	57.1	18.3	77.1	34.3
Shipbuilding and marine engineering	38.2	26.2	83.6	31.3
Vehicles	64.0	31.3	79.4	39.5
Metal goods not elsewhere specified	40.0	12.1	65.5	23.8
Textiles	38.9	10.2	72.2	26.7
Leather, leather goods, and fur	17.1	5.8	48.0	16.7
Clothing and footwear	32.3	7.3	52.8	14.9
Bricks, pottery, glass, cement, etc.	43.9	15.2	69.9	25.1
Timber, furniture, etc.	22.1	7.8	48.0	15.1
Paper, printing, and publishing	59.7	20.8	67.2	31.7
Other manufacturing industries	50.7	12.7	66.7	24.2
Total manufacturing industries	55.7	17.6	73.4	31.7
Non-manufacturing industries				
Agriculture, forestry, and fishing	19.9	4.9	56.2	19.6
Mining and quarrying	92.3	60.1	89.8	66.7
Construction	21.3	10.4	57.5	16.1
Gas, electricity, and water	76.2	62.8	93.8	80.1
Transport and communications	65.5	43.5	78.5	58.4
Distribution trades	38.1	9.7	50.0	14.5
Insurance, banking, finance, and business	76.4	35.7	83.2	47.1
Professional and scientific services	74.4	45.5	81.6	75.9
Miscellaneous services	29.5	8.9	50.3	23.6
Public administration	70.6	44.2	90.1	73.3
Total non-manufacturing industries	55.7	30.9	75.1	51.7
ALL INDUSTRIES AND SERVICES	54.4	26.4	74.5	47.4

Source: NES (Department of Employment Gazette, August 1971).

Membership and Non-membership of Occupational Pension Schemes, April 1970

	Numbers in millions	
Persons employed by private sector employers having pension schemes:		
Members		
Non-manual men	3.0	
women	0.9	
Manual men	2.6	
women	0.5	
		7.0
Non-members		
Too young	1.6	
Service too short but not too young	1.6	
Too old	0.3	
Employment ineligible	3.7	
Refused to join	0.7	
Other reasons	0.1	
		8.0
		15.0
Persons employed by public sector employers having pension schemes		5.8
		20.8
Persons employed by employers not having pension schemes		1.9
Total number of employed persons		22.7

Source: Tables 1, 2, and 3 in Occupational Pension Schemes 1971—Fourth Survey by the Government Actuary.

A Glossary of Terms

Pensions and Social Security legislation, together with pensions in general, have produced a range of expressions and abbreviations with special meanings. It is hoped this glossary will be of assistance to those involved in learning the jargon.

Actuary. An expert on pensions planning and design who is qualified to calculate the cost and value of benefits. A more general definition is indicated in the Institute of Actuaries publication, *The Actuarial Profession,* by the statement: "the essential function of an actuary is to apply the mathematical theory of probability, the theory of compound interest and statistical techniques to all manner of practical problems."

Additional component. That part of the State retirement pension which is earnings-related. It is derived from earnings between the *lower earnings limit* and the *upper earnings limit* at a rate of 1¼% per year from April 1978 for a maximum of 20 years, i.e. 25%. Where there are more than 20 years to be taken into account the highest 20 years' earnings will count. (Social Security Pensions Act 1975.)

Additional voluntary contributions. *See* AVC.

Administrator. The person or persons responsible for the management of an exempt approved scheme.

Allotment. (or **Allocation**). Setting aside a proportion of a member's pension to provide a dependant's pension.

Annuity. A regular fixed payment (pension) made for life or some other prescribed period, e.g. guaranteed for 5 years.

Assignment. The legal transference of property (pension benefits) to another person or persons.

Augmentation. Increasing the amount of normal pension entitlement either whilst it is accumulating or whilst in payment.

AVC. Additional voluntary contributions paid by a member to increase his retirement pension. AVCs plus normal contributions must not exceed 15% of earnings, nor must the total occupational pension being secured exceed two-thirds of final salary.

Average salary scheme. A pension scheme under which pensions are calculated upon average pensionable salary throughout membership. The additional component of the State retirement pension is a form of average salary scheme.

Basic component. That part of the retirement pension which derives from the basic State scheme, being the same as the single person's flat-rate State pension. It is intended that the basic component shall be increased annually in line with the movement in prices or national average earnings, whichever has risen most. (Social Security Pensions Act 1975.)

Centralised schemes. A centralised or federated scheme is one which embraces several employers who may or may not be associated.

Club, The. This arrangement was established to facilitate transfers of benefits between public service and nationalised industries' schemes. The system, also called the *Transfer Club,* has been extended so that private companies can participate.

Commutation. Exchanging a proportion of pension benefits for a lump sum within prescribed Inland Revenue limitations.

Contracted-out employment. An employment in relation to which a contracting-out certificate is in force. (Social Security Pensions Act 1975.)

Contracting out. Obtaining the approval of the Occupational Pensions Board for the members of an occupational scheme to opt out of the benefits provided by the earnings-related State scheme, i.e. the additional component, as a result of which lower rates of contributions are payable to the State. (The term *contracting out* (Social Security Pensions Act 1975) also applied to non-participating employments under the State Graduated Pension Scheme which was terminated on 5 April 1975.)

Contracting-out certificate. A certificate issued by the Occupational Pensions Board once it is satisfied the scheme meets the requirements of the Pensions Act and associated regulations. Notice has to be issued under the Contracts of Employment Act 1972 as to whether in respect of that employment a contracting-out certificate is in force. (Social Security Pensions Act 1975.)

Contributory scheme. A pension scheme in which members make normal contributions towards providing their pensions.

Controlled funding. *Controlled, adaptable, flexible,* or *planned funding* are terms descriptive of methods used to determine the percentage rate of contributions to a pension fund.

Declaration of trust. The formal written declaration of an employer setting out the establishment of a retirement benefits scheme under irrevocable trusts.

Dynamism. *See* Inflation proofing.

Earning factor. These are the earnings in any relevant tax year on which an earner pays contributions to the State.

Eligibility. The Rules of a pension scheme set out the membership qualifications which employees must have before being admitted, e.g. minimum and maximum ages of entry, minimum length of service, and category of employment.

Equal access. The Pensions Act 1975 requires that membership of occupational schemes (whether or not they are contracted out) shall be open to both male and female employees on identical terms of eligibility.

Escalation of pensions in payment. *See* Inflation proofing.

Exempt approved scheme. A scheme approved under the Finance Act 1970 which is shown to the satisfaction of the Inland Revenue to be established under irrevocable trust.

Final salary scheme. A pension scheme under which normal retirement pensions are calculated on a definition of earnings at or near to retirement, e.g. the average salary for the last 3 years, or average of the 3 highest consecutive years' earnings in the last 13 years of service.

Funding. The term given to meeting the cost of pension benefits under a scheme during members' active employment. Under an unfunded scheme pensions are paid out of income, described as the "pay-as-you-go" method.

Graduated pensions. The amounts of pension earned by contributions to the State Graduated Pension Scheme to April 1975 at which date benefits accrued under the scheme were frozen.

Group life assurance. This normally relates to lump-sum death-in-service benefits, the maximum amount approvable by the Inland Revenue being the greater of £5000 or four times final salary.

Guaranteed minimum pension (GMP) (*see also* Requisite benefits). The minimum benefit requirement to enable an occupational scheme to be contracted out. (Social Security Pensions Act 1975.)

Inflation proofing. Also called *dynamism* and *escalation*. Protecting the value of a pension against cost of living increases by periodic increases in benefits.

Inland Revenue approval.

(a) *Under the Income Tax Act 1952 (Old Code)*

The agreement by the Inland Revenue Authorities that a pension scheme meets all their requirements and that, in consequence members and employer will obtain appropriate tax reliefs. In the case of a Section 379 scheme, any United Kingdom tax deducted from investment income will be refunded by the Revenue Authorities. The employer's contributions are treated as an expense of management for tax purposes. Members' contributions to a Section 379 scheme are treated as expenses deductible from gross income and members' contributions to a Section 388 scheme or to an excepted provident fund obtain the same income tax relief as life assurance premiums. *All old code schemes must be amended as necessary to gain approval under the Finance Act 1970 before April 1980.*

(B) *(New Code)*

Under the Finance Act 1970 (as amended by the Finance Act 1971). This is obtainable under two alternatives: (i) obligatory approval by the Inland Revenue Authorities because the benefits comply with the somewhat restricted "prescribed conditions" set out in Section 19(2) and (2)(a) Finance Act 1970 as amended by the Finance Act 1971; (ii) "Discretionary approval" where the benefits comply with the less onerous Section 20(2) Finance Act 1970 as amended by the Finance Act 1971. Most schemes are granted approval under (ii). If Inland Revenue Approval is not forthcoming the employer's contributions will normally be treated as additional remuneration paid to employees, i.e. as an expense of management from the employer's point of view but as a taxable increase in remuneration from the member's point of view. An exempt approved scheme secures the same relief from taxation as a Section 379 fund.

Inland Revenue restrictions. Certain restrictions on contributions and on the amount and nature of benefits at retirement, death, or withdrawal which must be observed to secure approval to a pension scheme by the Inland Revenue Authorities.

Insured scheme. A scheme which is financed through premiums paid to an insurance company which then guarantees to pay the benefits provided under the scheme's rules.

Interim trust deed. A Section 379 pension scheme and certain exempt approved schemes are governed by a trust deed with a full set of rules. There is rarely time for legal advisers to agree to the trust deed and rules prior to commencement of a scheme and, therefore, an interim trust deed is executed setting up the trust, appointing trustees, and binding the employer within 12 months (or 2 years) to execute a definitive deed of trust which will confirm the trust set up and will set out in full the rules to be observed by trustees, employer, and members. The trust must be irrevocable.

Lower earnings limit. This is the approximate equivalent of the basic component (single person's flat-rate pension) in force at the commencement of an income tax year. (Social Security Pensions Act 1975.)

Money purchase scheme. A pension scheme under which the amounts of the pension benefits are determined by the contributions paid by and on behalf of each member, i.e. the contributions govern the benefits which are dependent upon the age of each individual member.

New code approval. *See* Inland Revenue approval.

Normal retirement age. This is the scheme's normal retirement age as specified in its rules which may be lower or higher than the State pension age.

Occupational Pensions Board (OPB). The Board, established by the Social Security Act 1973, generally supervises the pension rights and treatment of members, e.g. preservation entitlements. Under the Pensions Act 1975 the OPB is required to supervise the contracting-out procedures and supervise the solvency of contracted-out schemes.

Old code approval. *See* Inland Revenue approval.

Orphan's benefit. A pension payable to a member's orphan normally ceasing when the child attains age 18 or 21, and in some schemes, if later, on the termination of full-time education.

Past service pension. Usually defined to mean a pension in respect of a member's service prior to becoming a member of a current occupational scheme.

Pension. An annuity commencing on retirement payable for life. Many schemes provide in the rules for the pension to be guaranteed for 5 years, e.g. in the event of death within 5 years after retirement provision is made for a capital sum to be payable equal to the value of the pension instalments for the remainder of the 5-year period.

Pensionable earnings. Under a scheme's rules the amount of earnings upon which contributions and benefits are based.

Pensionable service. Service which counts towards entitlement to the scheme's benefits.

Preservation (*see also* Preservation requirements and Qualifying service for preservation). Maintaining a member's pension rights earning during his employment period when he leaves the scheme. The penson may be kept in the scheme, i.e. "frozen", or transferred to a new scheme.

Preservation requirements. A scheme must preserve those benefits which an early leaver has already earned and would be entitled to receive on retirement at the scheme's normal pension age. These include benefits in pension and lump-sum form and death benefits applying to death after normal pension age.

Qualifying service for preservation. A member who has attained age 26 and has completed 5 years of qualifying service must be offered the right to receive a preservation of benefits, i.e. the pension earned to date of leaving service. The 5 years may be pensionable service under the company scheme, recognised pensionable employment, service in another scheme linked by a transfer, or a combination of these.

Relevant benefits. Any pension, lump sum, gratuity, or other like benefit given or to be given on retirement, or death, or in anticipation of retirement, or, in connection with past service, after retirement or death, or to be given on or in anticipation of or in connection with any change in the nature of the service of the employee in question, except that it does not include any benefit which is to be afforded solely by reason of the disablement by accident of a person occurring during his service or of his death by accident so occurring and for no other reason. (This is the Finance Act of 1970 definition.)

Requisite benefits (*see also* Guaranteed minimum pension). These are the minimum benefits a scheme must provide to qualify for a contracted-out certificate. The scheme must be based on a final salary or a revalued average salary formula and provide a minimum pension accrual rate of 1¼%, i.e. 1/80th for each year of service after April 1978. (Social Security Pensions Act 1975.)

Retirement benefits scheme. A scheme for the provision of benefits consisting of or including relevant benefits.

Scale scheme. A pension scheme with the pension benefits set out in a table showing the amount of pension for each year of service in specified salary grades.

Section 379 scheme. A pension scheme approved by the Inland Revenue Authorities under Section 379 of the Income Tax Act 1952. The investment income of the pension scheme is free of United Kingdom tax, and contributions of members and employer are allowed as an expense. The scheme must be set up under a formal deed of trust and pensions are non-commutable at retirement unless of a trifling amount or in cases of extreme ill health. This section has been re-enacted under Section 208 Income and Corporation Taxes Act 1970.

Section 388 scheme. A pension scheme set up under Section 388 of the Income Tax Act 1952. Investment income is not tax free; the employer's contributions are allowed as an expense and members' contributions obtain the same tax relief as if they were life assurance premiums. Pensions are commutable at retirement to the extent that provided not less than three-quarters of the value of all pension benefits for a member are taken in the form of pension, the remaining quarter can be commuted for cash and if this quarter is the only pension provided by the Section 388 scheme (the three-quarters being provided by a 379 scheme) then it is wholly commutable. This section has been re-enacted under Section 222 of the Income and Corporation Taxes Act 1970.

Self-administered scheme (also known as a *private fund*). A scheme which is financed through investment by the trustee(s) direct, usually with the aid of an investment manager or with professional investment expertise. The pension benefits are not reassured by a life insurance company.

State pension age. Male 65 years, female 60 years.

Transfer value. When an employee leaves one pensionable employment and joins another with the rules of both schemes providing for transferability the cash equivalent of the member's accrued benefits is moved to the new scheme.

Transferability. The opportunity to transfer the cash equivalent of a member's accrued benefits when moving to a new scheme. Comparable benefits are then provided in the new scheme.

Unit scheme. This is a scheme under which a member is entitled to a pension of £x per annum for each year of pensionable service.

Unit-linked scheme. A scheme which is invested, wholly or in part, in unit trusts managed by an insurance company, merchant or joint stock bank, or similar financial institution.

Upper earnings limit. This is approximately seven times the lower earnings limit. (Social Security Pensions Act 1975.)

Valuation. *Actuarial valuation*—the regular examination and report on a pension fund by an actuary to ensure that it has adequate assets to meet the liabilities (the cost of the benefits). *Stock market valuation*—the market values of a pension fund's assets as compared with book values (usually cost prices) on predetermined accounting dates or on the date appropriate to the periodic actuarial valuation.

Widow's/Widower's pension option (*see also* Allotment). A member's right to give up part of his/her pension to provide a spouse's pension.

Index